Best Wishes,
Jane Fox

The Hungry Mother

Recipes for Recovery and Life in the Kitchen

Jane Fox

Published October 2022

ISBN: 979-8-9856298-7-3
Library of Congress Control Number: 2022914665

For information address:
The Three Tomatoes Book Publishing
6 Soundview Rd.
Glen Cove, NY 11542
www.thethreetomatoespublishing.com

Cover design: Susan Herbst
Cover photograph: Vasyl Dolmatov, iStock
Interior design: Susan Herbst

Dedication

To my daughters, Teddie and Paige, whose love, laughter,
and tears are a beacon of light on my journey.

And to the memories of family members,
whose sense of humor in the face of adversity was
served warm at the dinner table.

And to mothers in recovery and the children who wait for them.
Never give up; recovery is always possible.

Table of Contents

Introduction

The legend of Hungry Mother takes many forms, and all have whispers of the truth. The one widely accepted by the people of Southwest Virginia goes like this...

> *A pioneer named Molly Marley and her small child were captured by a Native American tribe and taken to their mountain camp. Molly and her little one escaped, wandering into the woods, finding shelter in an abandoned cabin. Eventually, a search party discovered Molly dead from starvation and the daughter uttering the words "hungry mother," pointing to a pile of berries and nuts. Legend has it that the mother sacrificed herself to keep her child alive.*
>
> *~from the website I Love Virginia State Parks,*
> *www.dcr.virginia.gov/state-parks/hungry-mother*
> *The Hungry Mother Park, located in Marion, Virginia*

I heard the story of Molly Marley several years ago. It stayed with me and inspired the title of this book. The Hungry Mother is a perfect metaphor for sober moms who are navigating sobriety using culinary activities to enrich relationships with our children and ourselves. Throughout this book, you will discover the significant connection between cooking and recovery, complete with parenting tips, quotes, and recipes.

In my forty years of sobriety over forty-five years, it was the falling out and coming back as a sober mom, a Hungry Mother, that marks my spirituality. Ten years ago, with my daughters grown up, the empty nest syndrome was challenging my sobriety. It was only a matter of time before I fell completely. I needed an intervention ASAP, and having recovery credentials, I came up with this sober plan—move to South Florida and manage transitional residences for women.

Over the next five years, I witnessed the positive impact of culinary activities on recovering people, activities that had also worked for me. Raising my daughters after relapsing, I relied on cooking to reconnect, regain authority, and over time, uphold their trust. In transitional living, residents aspire to replace a lifetime of bad habits and life-threatening pleasures; what better vehicle than the culinary experience to learn a healthy balance?

At the start of transitional living, there is an urgent need to change gears. Recovering people are starving for a life that matters, praying it's not just something to be endured as the odds of staying sober under those conditions are slim. Daily cooking grows into developing good habits. Over time, the cooking experience accumulates into a bank account of life-affirming activities, integral to sustaining sobriety.

While there, I witnessed firsthand how recovering people who embraced culinary activities seemed better equipped to sustain sobriety. Following the directions of a recipe is parallel to taking the steps for sustaining sobriety. These simple culinary transactions translate directly to the recovery experience, as the ingredients for early sobriety include treatment, 12-step meetings, and a sober support community. The steps for making a meal is a process that requires planning, preparation, and clean-up, in essence, mirroring a 12-step structure. There are no shortcuts or skipping corners as the results would be inedible.

The ritual of food preparation becomes an exercise in self-preservation. On an innate level, it taps into the resilient nature within us all. In essence, it's a way to reconnect with the nascent compass of survival versus self-destruction, hunger, or satiation. One is either moving toward or away from recovery, growing or regressing. Creating rituals we design makes them easier to adhere to, and at the end of the day, we can look back and take pride in our actions.

Hungry Mothers are lucky. We have a reason other than ourselves to sustain sobriety, our children. We don't want to fail and leave them an inheritance of dysfunction, disappointment, and an anguished destiny.

Hope sings softly in women's 12-step meetings. In recovery, mothers are on a maternal mission. The pull of motherhood is an amazing advantage, not the liability first imagined. There's an anthropological purpose in staying sober, a primal reminder of a greater good—other lives are at stake. We listen hard, sharing stories on sacred ground. Personal differences are bridged by aha moments, but it's the communal laughter of women that moves me the most. It shines a certain brightness on what we face, helping to change perspective.

Over time, I realized that recovery is emancipation, not a prison sentence. Sober, life was no longer tangled with high drama, giving time to find joy and comfort. Simple interests, close at hand, brought a steady hum of satisfaction. Cultivating interests that define me brought me into the world—eventually growing into a new role, a woman with interests, an interesting woman.

Finding healthy pleasures in sobriety is serious business, as the consequences of insufficient amounts inevitably lead to recidivism. Culinary activities stimulate the creative process for individual expression. It is a chance to experiment with personal preferences at no risk and to connect with sober peers. Cultivating hobbies and interests are stepping stones to life-affirming behavior, essential for long-term recovery.

Overcoming addiction gives us the freedom to recognize our imperfections, misdeeds, and vulnerabilities; we've learned to own and befriend them. By hitting bottom, we gain humility, integrity, and wholeness, finally seeing that sobriety is a life-affirming experience, not one of embarrassment and shame but a blessing in disguise.

> *The genius of love and the genius of hunger, those twin brothers, are the two moving forces behind all living things. All living things set themselves in motion to feed and to reproduce. Love and hunger share the same purpose. Life must never cease, life must be sustained and must create.*
>
> *~Turgenev, Russian novelist, 1850s*

My hope is to spark sober moms to become Hungry Mothers and take advantage of the culinary activities that saved me while cementing the bonds of motherhood, family, and those we love. It's a roadmap that painstakingly charts the course of a mother's recovery, over forty-five years of sobriety and relapse, and serves as proof to never give up.

And to family members with a loved one struggling with substance abuse, my message is, there is hope. Shining light on the tragic, gritty reality of substance abuse goes to "break the stigma and start a conversation." Encouraging dialogue leads to a better understanding of alcoholism and addiction and contributes to the solution. Every community has a profound capacity to help. It is time to "bring recovery up from the basement and into the kitchen."

Keep on cooking!
Jane Fox, the Hungry Mother

We cannot control the wind.
We can only adjust the sails.

~Cora L.V. Hatch, well-known medium
of the Spiritualism movement, 1859

Chapter 1

Courage to Get Sober
One Meal at a Time

"Progress in civilization has been accompanied by progress in cookery."
~ Fanny Farmer, American culinary expert

Addiction put a hard edge on my personality. I was a master at rationalization and wishful thinking—denial and minimization ruled. Logical thinking was interrupted, overtaken by addictive thinking as my strung-out behavior replaced healthy, normal judgment. How else to continue addiction in the face of accumulating consequences? I was on a treadmill of hustling and lying, taking risks every day. The shady lady in me mistook crime for adventure and walked on the wild side to get what I needed.

Ironically, in early abstinence, those outlaw traits served me well, and there's an important theory, the preferred defense structure (PDS), which explains the twisted logic from the perspective of an addict/alcoholic. Navigating a dysfunctional life still requires a system of logic and beliefs—the career addict/alcoholic uses it to maneuver through the elements of a strung-out life. Deliberate denial of certain life difficulties is a useful temporary adjustive device. I did it for years. "Denying" the truth, and that attitude of denial can be used as a coping mechanism, translating to a positive force in early recovery.

> ...*none* [in reference to various alcoholism therapy approaches] *have taken into account the attributes,*

characteristics, and common situational elements of the alcoholic and the alcoholic career. ...the preferred defense structure (PDS) of the recovering alcoholic can be used effectively to produce initial abstinence.

~John Wallace, PhD, addiction specialist

There's a hidden value in the behavior addicts utilize; a certain boldness and bravery are needed to score. For me, that junkie attitude, the collection of skills and strategies, became an ally in early recovery. Felony still lived in my heart—it's impossible to abandon old behaviors. We can't go from bad to good overnight. That junkie attitude continues through early abstinence. It's to be expected, but it doesn't signal recovery isn't working. Changing hard-wired attitudes of addiction takes time, focus, and determination, something the recovering addict/alcoholic has little of.

*****

1972, Tucson

With careful planning, I could drive the backroads from Tucson to Aspen in twenty-four hours. Riding shotgun with Senta, transporting one hundred kilos of weed stashed beneath the trunk panel, this was my virgin voyage. Crisscrossing Indian reservations on a Friday night, my job was to look out for pick-up trucks driving home from cashing paychecks at the liquor store, drunk. Traveling through northeast Arizona, interstates were not an option as state troopers were on alert—only the most treacherous routes late at night served our purpose best.

Each passing mile of the desert valley and winding blacktop became a revelation of Senta's rituals. She was a dust bowl angel with the gumption of a Wall Street heavy hidden behind Keene doll eyes. At 5'10", with strawberry-blonde hair and eyelashes to match, she traveled hard with the fast crowd, daring dudes cashing in on the early days of the marijuana trade. She could sweep a man off his feet by walking into a room, but make no mistake, she kept a portfolio on each one—where their mother lived, sexual proclivity, and favored firearm. She was all business, and I was the amazed and grateful apprentice to this underground union for $ 1,000 per trip.

An adventurous winter break from college brought me to the University of Boulder to visit a friend from high school. On a whim, we decided to rendezvous with other friends at the University of Tucson and drove all night, stopping only for gas. Upon arrival, I called on a mad crush from the University of Pittsburgh, who like many young men, skipped the East Coast seeking to avoid the draft for the Vietnam War and changed his name. Enrolled in architecture at the university, he was living with a bunch of people at Eleven Arches, off River Road in the Catalina Foothills of the Old Pueblo, and invited me to visit.

Nothing prepared me for the massive adobe estate with mosaic reflecting pools nestled among kumquat trees and multi-toned hummingbirds. Two gatehouses flanked the quarter-mile driveway to the main house, complete with tie-dye banners floating out of the windows. Originally, it was the Grace estate of the steamship family, built in the early twenties, to satisfy a bohemian daughter who was tired of the continent and discovered the solitude of the American Southwest like Georgia O'Keefe. No expense was spared, and the sprawling stucco walls encapsulated several wings and outbuildings. Now, it housed a loosely related group of people, as only the early seventies could—the most divine commune imaginable!

The decision to move out west was easy. Hungover with the humiliation of the first of many psychiatric hospitalizations for substance abuse, a change in location was the perfect solution.

I had been a nursing student at the University of Pittsburgh, a five-year program in four, and if you failed a course, you had to wait one year until it was offered again. Having mastered the class on injections and syringes, I utilized those skills to try heroin. By junior year, my recreational use had turned addictive, with schoolwork suffering and my folks growing suspicions, resulting in mandated psychotherapy at college or returning home. Through "Jewish geography," they found Dr. Hazel, a Freudian analyst whose office was conveniently located in the lobby of Western Psychiatric, part of the nursing rotation. Four days a week during my lunch break, I would lay on the proverbial "analyst couch," avec uniform and cap, while Dr. Hazel asked questions in true Freudian fashion out of view.

Part of me sensed danger and admitted the truth to Dr. Hazel, who in turn recommended a voluntary admission in the wing located three floors up. Turned out, "voluntary" translated into three months while nursing peers stared at me from the other side of the locked door. I felt complete humiliation, disgrace, and shame. Finally discharged, I moved home and enrolled at C.W. Post College. After visiting Tucson that spring, I needed no convincing or concrete plans to move there, flying back to Long Island long enough to pack up my car and dog and skipping out on final exams.

In 1972, Tucson was an odd combination of frontier and college town. Flavors of the Old West dotted the landscape, and the university attitude mimicked a Jack Kerouac novel. The stunning northern Sonoran Desert, neatly framed by mountain ranges on three sides, was where the commune had a restaurant, The Hungry Mother Café, where I first heard the story of the Hungry Mother. I settled in with a job, a new boyfriend, and a storybook place to live. Here, being a college dropout with a shady past of drug abuse held no shame. It was in sharp contrast to the loser I felt like back East among family and accomplished high school friends.

Downtown Tucson's Fifth Street was lined with stores owned by guys whose nicknames blended into dubious career paths. Turquoise Lenny, Wayne's Leathers, Zips' Records—such establishments formed an economy founded by draft dodgers and pot dealers, where no one used their true name, as big money was made and spent. It made all those "desirable" JAPs (Jewish American Princes) from Great Neck seem like wimps.

These dealers were sexy in their pearl-snap shirts and genuine cowboy boots, riding around in shiny pick-up trucks—dogs in the back, tongues hanging for water. They were mysterious, too, with lots of cash to go around for restaurant dinners of twenty guests—the fast crowd of pot-smuggling cowboys bearing gifts of Indian jewelry and safe houses hidden in the desert. Melt my heart, it was the land of milk and honey, and I was game. *Yeehaw!*

Eventually, Senta's steady driving lulled the thought of the kilos from my consciousness, an essential attitude for this business. At five a.m., sleep deprivation fueled a sensation of spiritual awareness. Seeing the sunrise over the Painted Desert preserve brought me to a visionary chapter in my life. The "Folly of Youth" and its sequel, "How to Live Above the Laws of God and Man Without Getting Busted," were required reading for so many of us then. Snorting coke off Senta's curved pinky fingernail, a must-have accessory, fueled my fantasy. It was the final launch sequence, catapulting me into an orbit of substance abuse where logistics for re-entry had not been fully calculated. *What was the name of that astronaut's college?*

The conversation turned sporadic, and we talked of how we'd spend the money, the men we slept with, the moves they made, the drugs they offered. Senta reminisced about the finale of her last run, crowned with celebrity status by the "reception" committee waiting at Jerome Hotel's bar. In the seventies, pot dealers were the rock stars of Aspen, and the couriers, bold young women, an asset to promote and protect.

"It's a double-edged sword," she quietly lectured. "You're greeted at the door by your backer, beaming with good judgment, thrilled you earned him $50,000 in a single haul. But find a quiet moment and search his eyes for that hidden glimmer, a silent code of affirmation. If you ever burned him, are short on poundage, or give up his name, he'll hunt you down. Learn it, memorize it, don't ever forget it."

She was a cornucopia of information, providing tricks of the trade and nuggets of survival secrets, not all of which were unpleasant. How to party with clients without getting too stoned to drive home, and never get into bed with a backer until the job was done and cash changed hands. She shot me a sobering look. "The best insurance policy is intimacy, so sleep with him at some point. A lover will hesitate before hurting, buying time to escape by words or action." Pulling up a bell-bottomed pant leg, she revealed an abalone shell snub-nose .38 strapped against her delicate ankle. "My back-up policy." And in a twinkling of an Okie laugh and a flutter of those luscious, strawberry-blonde lashes, she passed the mantle onto me.

Senta, now silent, pulled on leather driving gloves so sweat wouldn't loosen her grip on the wheel. Great lament welled up behind my over-stimulated eyeballs as I envisioned the headlines in the *Great Neck Record,* "Body of local girl recovered in Colorado ravine." We pressed upward on a two-lane road, reaching Red Mountain Pass at 11,000 feet, and then descended. As we passed through Silverton and Ouray, Victorian ghost towns and a rumored art colony, a low-hanging cloud cover masked the road in front. Now headed downhill for 5,000 feet, brakes squeaking as our cargo shifted in the trunk, we slowly coasted down to the desert plateau below. My heart and stomach lurched in silent tandem with each passing mile.

And then suddenly, the sun burst through my tears as the lush magnificence of Montrose's agricultural valley appeared in the distance. *God is good! Yeehaw!* Falling out of the car at the first gas station, complete with a farm stand, we embraced like survivors from a shipwreck. Early evening light chased the cold hand of fear long enough to buy pounds of local peaches and PAYDAY bars before tearing off into the oncoming dusk in the home stretch to A-town.

*****

It was a pivotal psychic moment. The spiritual calm of conquering death-defying illegal feats, financial reward, and notoriety affirmed a lopsided logic. This would result in several psychiatric hospitalizations and a year-long stint in a therapeutic community for heroin addiction and another six months of re-entry. There is nothing more perilous than surviving near-fatal experiences to empower a whacked-out code of ethics.

I embraced the proverb of '70s drug culture: "Bite the bullet of good judgment, keep wits, and get out of town under cover of the night." Overcome with accomplishment, never experienced scholastically or socially, sealed the deal. Hook, line, and syringe. Finally, I felt special and smart with entry to an exclusive club. The music, outfits, attitudes, and anti-social behavior of the '70s legitimized my theory. I was on top of the corporate ladder and walked with attitude in cowgirl boots of hand-tooled leather.

Living life on the edge is risky, and copping drugs have symptoms too: heart pounding, mind-racing, self-loathing, and the physical discomfort of being strung out. Walking into a 12-step meeting and admitting my recovery reality felt remarkably similar. In "active" addiction, I'd wake up each morning in a panic, emotionally and physically, and against all odds, "achieved" the goal of getting high. In early abstinence, I felt the same panic. How would I get through the day without using? Tapping into that upside-down courage, the preferred defense system (PDS), helped me achieve abstinence. Before, I was willing to go to any lengths to get high; now I had to do the opposite. The possibility of losing custody gave me the guts to push through. If I had the "courage" to be active, why not flip it around to commit to sobriety?

Projection of blame and intellectualization are coping tactics needed for the anxiety-laden, guilt-provoking experiences to sustain our habits. It also provides an escape from the emotional consequences of substance abuse, a form of denial. Those defense mechanisms now worked in my favor, helping me ignore the stigma of being in recovery. After all, I was immune to the comments and opinions of others when active. Paradoxically, it becomes a straightforward shift from rationalizing substance abuse to rationalizing other less than desirable behaviors with sobriety.

As a single mother of two young daughters, the ability to mask fear to the law, a dealer, or strung-out junkie converted into positive life skills. "It's okay, sweet girlies, Mommy has everything under control. There's nothing to be afraid of." Oh, yeah, but what if I was terrified too? I made jokes, teasing my daughters out of scary moments, making light when I was filled with fear or distress. It would calm everyone down temporarily, giving me time to collect my wits and think of a solution.

Late-night thunderstorms swayed our one-hundred-year-old Victorian house as wind gusts off Long Island Sound banged loose gutters and screens. Our bodies locked together in my king-sized bed, tummy to tushy for physical reassurance.

"Let's count the seconds between lightning and the boom to measure how far away the storm is," I'd say. Distraction, I realized, was key.

"Mommy, what's that noise? It sounds like the front door slammed open and someone's inside!" whispered the youngest in fright one evening.

Jokingly, I responded, "Sweetie, you're confusing it with the horror movie we rented from Blockbuster last week."

"No, Mom," replied older sister in her best Valley Girl voice, "you're thinking of the one where evil spirits travel through the shower drain and take control over the children's bodies."

"Then they kill all the parents in town?" the youngest answered conspiratorially.

"Yeah, that's the one."

Geez, I hate scary movies! I'm not afraid of robbers, burglars, or malicious males, only the imaginary monster living in the basement and the Creature from the Blue Lagoon. Things that go bump in the night seemed real to me, and I refused to watch flicks that celebrated them. Secretly, I agreed with my daughter—it did sound like the frigging front door, but what was a mother to do? At least I got her to change the subject. The only problem was, now I was the one who was scared.

Fresh from divorce, I'd swallow my fear with a pill to calm down. That warm fuzzy feeling eliminated the uncomfortable challenge of being responsible for my young family's security and locking up every night. I rationalized my situation away, needing extra courage for those unexpected responsibilities. Late-night dialogues swirled in my head, and I awakened each morning with an anxiety attack big enough to immobilize a small army. *Maybe take another pill?* my mind would suggest.

Over time, I learned to keep a variety of blunt, seemingly harmless objects by the doors and under the bed, a homemade arsenal. It brought a sense of security, and I learned to put faith in my emotional strength rather than pharmaceuticals. My prized possession was my grandfather's hand-carved wood shillelagh, probably NYPD, circa 1900. Being prepared eliminated half the anxiety—true for all things. The reckless courage of addiction translated to the bravery of sustaining recovery and single parenthood.

*****

Hungry Mother Tips

- Adrenaline is a hormonal rush. Go with the flow. It's empowerment on a cellular level.
- Never admit to being afraid at the time of the event; save that for future discussion with other adults.
- Reward yourself after each encounter with the sweetest food in the house.

Benefit Of Cooking

Cooking a new recipe requires courage, taking on a special meaning and urgency in early recovery. Following a recipe is an exercise in patience, preparation, and fruition, closely mirroring the 12 steps. We come to each dish without specific culinary knowledge, only the hope and faith that it will be delicious.

In cooking, variables are unavoidable, and responding to that unpredictability is a valuable trait in cooking. The key to good cooking is understanding the diversity of the ingredients and the boundless range of possible outcomes.

Recipes don't tell us everything; they are not prescriptions, only helpful over-the-back-fence suggestions, as if we already know how to make the dish. It can feel risky, even treacherous, to take on, but in reality, it is an exercise in free will and self-determination. Sustaining sobriety relies on our ability to make bold and brave choices every day, reflecting a new way of thinking.

Making a new dish is an ideal exercise to increase our confidence in taking healthy risks. Accumulating cooking experiences improved my judgment in all capacities, a culinary safety net. For example, onions have many ways of being prepped—whole or in quarters, sliced thick or thin, chopped, diced, or minced—and can be cooked fast, slow, or caramelized.

> *The idea is to inform yourself well enough to make choices that make sense. Making a bunch of unruly ingredients behave themselves, work together and nourish, takes a leap of faith. Recipes ask us to apply thinking, intelligence and judgment to ideas and to the materials that will be turned into a dish. It is up to us to bring our own good sense to cooking while acknowledging our tastes and preferences.*
>
> *~Nach Waxman, Founder, Kitchen Arts & Letters*

All the ingredients needed for sober parenting. Take a chance; cook a challenging dish!

Hungry Mother Recipe: Oat Bran Yogurt Pancakes

I am always looking for a breakfast that packs a healthy punch, takes less than five minutes to assemble, and is low-calorie. Eating oat bran for breakfast regularly will help keep your family "regular." Enhance the healthy aspects by adding flax seed, wheat germ, or whatever else is in your arsenal. Store the mixture of oat bran, flaxseed, and wheat germ mixture in a large Mason jar for easy access. Collecting Mason jars at tag and garage sales is a hobby of mine, and I use them to brew sun tea, refrigerate iced coffee, or bring food to a friend.

Look for consistency somewhere between a pancake and crepe; the batter should be runny, not firm. I cook this as one large pancake. The fun begins when each person adds a favorite topping of powdered sugar or jam and finds a way to use that over-ripe banana.

Ingredients

1/2 cup plain Greek yogurt or flavored

1/2 cup egg white

Dash of vanilla (or almond or chocolate extract)

1/2 tsp cinnamon

1 packet sweetener (or 2 tsp sugar or 1 tbsp maple syrup)

1/3 - 1/2 cup oat bran mixture {flaxseed, wheat germ, or any other fiber-rich additive}

1 - 2 tsp oil (whatever is on hand); my preference is almond oil.

Non-stick pan, rubber spatula

Directions

1. Using a whisk, beat yogurt & egg white together.
2. Add in extract, cinnamon, and sweetener.
3. Whisk in oat bran mixture until all ingredients are blended.
4. Heat (medium) non-stick pan; coat or spray with oil.
5. Pour in pancake mixture and, holding the handle of the pan, gently shake so the batter sits evenly.
6. Cook until the open side starts to firm up and bubble 5-8 minutes then flip over. This batter is mostly liquid and needs longer than regular pancakes.

Use a spatula to check the underside of the pancake; it should be ready to flip when browned. Flip over and cook until the other side is browned. Leftovers stay fresh in the refrigerator and travel well if running out of the house. An after-breakfast snack to eat in the car!

Chapter 2

Break the Stigma

Judge Me by My Chicken Soup, Not My Past

...I, with my brain and my hands, have nourished my beloved few,
that I have concocted a stew or a story, a rarity or a plain dish,
to sustain them truly against the hungers of the world.
~MFK Fisher, American food writer

I came back into the rooms pushing a wheelbarrow of shame. My children watched me hit bottom and everything in between. They witnessed every nook and cranny of my addiction. Guilty visions of my strung-out behavior haunted me on the sleepless nights of early abstinence. The consequences of my actions could translate to losing custody, a future without them. I let that image linger. That vision motivated me to push through moments of wanting to give up and pick up. Now, sustaining sobriety is forever linked to repairing that wrong.

One night, desperate for a group, I took my youngest to a 12-step meeting. Uncertainty washed over us—for her, because she was surrounded by strangers, and for me, from the hesitation to qualify in front of her. A wave of motherhood swept through my sober heart. Aching to reassure that my addiction was in the past, it felt counter-intuitive to say "Jane, addict-alcoholic." I was Mommy again, working hard at my program, and deserved a positive spin. Hungry Mothers manage a universe of recovery, our own and that of our children, which takes twice the energy. Maternal drive boosted the sober spirit needed to carry my children along. That night I responded, "My name is Jane, and I'm a sober mom."

*****

1976, A Scream Away from Happiness

I was disgracefully discharged from Long Island Jewish Hillside, my fourth psychiatric hospitalization for substance abuse, and there was nothing new on the treatment horizon for addiction. Back in the '70s, the only drug rehabs were state-run places like Daytop, Phoenix House, and Synanon for addicts coming out of prison. The other option, mostly reserved for upscale junkies, was a psychiatric hospital where addiction was labeled as a mental illness.

Fed up and strung-out, in between programs and in true junkie fashion, I considered moving to Bangkok to satisfy my yen for heroin. One day, I let that idea slip to family. A few days later, on my twenty-fifth birthday, a creative intervention delivered me to the office of New York State's chief judge, Sol Wachtler, a family friend. The judge was reading my file when I walked into his chambers. I glanced at the plaques and photos hanging on the walls—this was serious. With only the two of us, he pronounced judgment, "Janie, either live for one year at AREBA, a therapeutic community in New York City, or I'll commit you upstate to a psychiatric hospital. Those are your only options."

The room got quiet. I flashed on jumping out of the car on the Long Island Expressway, rolling onto a shoulder, dusting myself off, then hitching a ride to JFK. Or, accepting my fate and living for a year with other upscale junkies in Manhattan—at least the pizza would be good. But first I had to detox. It was the bicentennial, July 4th, 1976, and the only facility taking patients was in Rockaway Beach. I arrived at rock bottom as the only female withdrawing among a dozen disenfranchised junkies.

Yankee Doodle went to detox
Feeling oh, so crappy
Stick a need in my arm and call me very happy.

Through barred windows, I watched tall ships sail toward the Statue of Liberty and families of all origins squeeze onto patches of scratchy sand, eating and laughing. All had lives brighter than mine. Visions of marriage, motherhood, celebrating a future fourth, were all possible if I stayed clean. One hundred years ago, my relatives, fleeing Europe for America, had that same view of Lady Liberty. I now wondered, *What's a nice Jewish girl from Great Neck doing here?* The floodgates opened, pushing regret, remorse, and guilt to the top of my consciousness. The possibility of a future appeared through those unwashed windows—the only requirement was not to pick up and move on. Swearing to all my immigrant relatives, I vowed never again.

The next day, walking into an elegant townhouse on East 52nd Street, I was greeted by collective screaming. Had I arrived in Hades? A therapy group was in session and echoed through the lobby. Tucked among corporate headquarters between Madison and Park was a thirty-bed drug rehab owned by Dr. Daniel Casriel. AREBA, an acronym for accelerated re-education of emotions, behavior, and attitude was the designated therapy at this private therapeutic community, which would be my home for the next year. Still, I wasn't prepared for the interview requiring me to qualify by crying out for help to my new family of recovering addicts, demanding emotional proof of my commitment.

Dr. Dan co-founded Daytop Village with Monsignor O'Brien, funded by New York State, the first therapeutic community of its kind on the East Coast. It had a solid reputation for long-term recovery and a waiting list. As a young psychiatrist working with ex-con addicts at Synanon (California), Dr. Dan witnessed the power of confrontation groups and peer pressure, which apparently yielded an incredible 80-percent success rate. Dr. Dan morphed that into the New Identity

Process and ushered in a new generation of therapeutic communities (TCs) onto the East Coast. Phoenix House and Odyssey followed and were highly effective for urban addicts but not for middle-class junkies. Dr. Dan discovered a niche market of privileged kids unable to bond with their brothers from the ghetto and started a private therapeutic community, blending therapeutic modalities.

A banking magnate's daughter ventured in a limo from the family's Park Avenue triplex to score heroin on 125th and Lennox. She had just broken up with her junkie boyfriend and was strung out. Arrested after addressing the pimps on the corner, "Uh, pardon me, know where I can cop some Mexican Mud?", the rest was history.

AREBA evolved into a blue-chip program for the strung-out offspring of the well-to-do. From real estate magnets and industry captains to entertainers and artists, these desperate folks gladly funded this venture. Dr. Dan's group psychotherapy was revolutionary, harnessing screaming, hugging, and affirmations of basic needs into a program of emotional recovery. Mat work, group sessions on mattresses scattered around the floor, were used to work out feelings of anger, fear, and pain. Screaming out bad feelings reduced volatility and the need for self-medication to manage desperate emotions. Weekly confrontation groups affected change in behavior and attitudes. Maximizing the therapeutic community dynamic, incorporating a military model of structure, and brilliantly utilizing emotional work on the mats led his patients to emotionally open up to accept good feelings. This unique therapeutic modality produced amazing results.

His book, *A Scream Away from Happiness*, gained notoriety with the New Identity Process, a psycho-dynamic therapy blending Gestalt therapy with the Jungian primal scream and a pinch of Freudian libido. All psychiatrists must go through analysis for training, and his was conducted by Dr. Abram Kardiner, Sigmund Freud's last student. That experience left an impression. AREBA gained traction in Europe too—Milan especially, where scores of young addicts from wealthy industrialist families were strung out just like they were in New York City. But in Italy, the mob was serious, selling them pure heroin, then making them an easy target for kidnapping. Rich, Northern Italians shipped their kids with cash to East 52nd Street, and by the time I got there, AREBA was filled with a wealthy, international clientele.

In 1976, *Network* won four Academy Awards, with Paddy Chayefsky receiving two for best screenplay and director. New Yorkers opened their windows, screaming, "I'm mad as Hell and I'm not going to take it anymore!" That declaration was inspired by his son's experience as an AREBA resident and by Paddy's personal experience attending groups. Dr. Dan achieved an amazing 85-percent success rate for those who completed the year's residential treatment, and five years later, nearly the same percentage remained drug-free.

That's me, forty-five years later—one of the lucky ones in that percentage, and that's why I continue to pass it on.

*****

1997, Take It to The Mats

The morning my twelve-year-old daughter was diagnosed with juvenile diabetes, a backwash of adrenaline swept through my organs. Heartbreaking, mind-racing, stomach-ulcerating ice water flowed through my veins. Hunched over in the corridor outside her hospital room, the still waters of reality settled over me after the hustle of an emergency admission. Just as her pancreas shut down, so did I. A single, sober mom, two years clean; how much could one person manage? They say God doesn't give more than you can handle, but this put me over the edge; I was overextended, ready to blow.

A day later, she was out of danger, and we began the educational component of controlling glucose levels, now a part of our lives forever. The nurse practitioner walked us through daily routines, ramifications, and dietary restrictions. Just when I thought my head would explode, syringes were demonstrated for loading and injecting insulin. Whoa—it was a homecoming reunion! The Sobriety God was proving an existential point! My wacky higher power transformed the nastiest, most shameful part of my past into an asset, a bizarre master plan.

Declining to share my familiarity with the nurse, a gong—nay, a stick of dynamite—went off in my head, letting me know there are no coincidences. As an ex-junkie, needles don't frighten me, a good thing because my daughter could read my face like a book and only saw calm. Silently, I suppressed a cryptic chortle as my higher power provided a comedic moment in the face of adversity. Karmic humor, laughter at the expense of my painful past, gave me courage and saved my butt.

A year later, juvenile diabetes had us both fearful and frustrated. For her, it was missing school and friends, and for me, it became impossible to maintain a career. One difficult day, the meter was acting wonky, offering different readings each time. Unable to determine how much insulin was needed meant another pharmacy run for a new meter. I felt like screaming and saw she did too. I flashed on smashing that meter. And so, we did. Carefully placing a beach towel underneath, we made a pile of all her broken meters and took turns hammering them to bits. Instant relief was followed by laughing, sobbing, and hugging, just like in an AREBA group. I began to look at recovery as something more than being sober, as representing emotional health that I could count on in any situation.

When I was active, I was always getting pulled over for speeding and would talk my way out of it. Now, ironically, I had license to speed, armed with doctor's cards, hospital phone numbers, and medic alert and business cards from work if I got pulled over racing home. "Officer, my daughter's a diabetic. The school nurse called. I'm on my way to pick her up," I said one day when pulled over, wearing panic like a favorite pair of flannel pajamas. "All right, lady, you can go this time, but a dead or crippled mom won't be of any help, so slow down," he had replied, handing back my license, registration, and insurance card—sans ticket.

God is good but certainly strange.

*****

Maternal instinct is a two-way street, and my children sensed something was wrong with Mommy. Denial, a driving force of addiction, made me a liar, deceiving them on every level. Intuitively knowing what is true and what is not is a precious gift, but my addictive behavior made mincemeat of their internal compass, robbing them of that skill. Pretending my erratic behavior never happened would be a tragic lie. It was time for honesty about my recovery.

The expectation to reconnect in a significant way only happened by talking about what went on between us. Being honest was an opportunity to account for past actions so we could move on. Children need to connect the dots and quietly put the pieces of the puzzle together. It gives them a chance to reconcile the past with the future and a reassurance that everything will be okay.

Recovery is emancipation, not a prison sentence. Breaking through the stigma of addiction is the first step of recovery, realizing it's a life-affirming experience, not one of embarrassment and shame. I confused the legitimate prejudice of addiction with who I am today. There's a difference between guilt and shame. One leads to corrective action, and the other to despair and resignation. Guilt can be changed by making amends, and cooking for my family was the perfect dish.

No matter how jagged or raw, family life is a sobriety safety net, a cradle to catch us from falling. Newly sober and attending meetings every day, I offered vague excuses for my absence; it felt reminiscent of addictive behavior. How many times did I disappear to pick up a prescription, nod out in my room, or behave erratically? Breaking anonymity with the family goes to preventing recidivism. Once they knew I was trying to stay sober, I didn't want to fail. At times, it added notes of levity as children love to chastise parents. "Mom, you're going to be late for your meeting!" Silently laughing to myself, I wondered, Who are you, my sponsor? Prescribed amounts of levity are necessary, as real life waits outside those basement rooms. Enough of the tears; a quiet chuckle feels better than crying. Even Buddha, upon attaining enlightenment, saw the value of humor within a suffering life. Each meeting ended with us holding hands, praying to return the following week.

*****

Hungry Mother Tips

- Take it to the mats. When children are overwhelmed by feelings, encourage them to "work it out on the mats" by crying and banging on pillows, a valuable emotional release. It's preferable over kicking holes into walls, anorexia, or self-cutting.
- Who's yelling the most, you or them? Recognize your own rising heat on the emotional thermometer and give yourself a time-out. Never underestimate the power of releasing emotions to self-calm. Soups, sauces, and feelings boil over; learn to lower the flame.
- The healing powers of chicken soup cannot be overrated. From heartache to head cold, it demonstrates caring compassion to the lucky recipient.

Benefit Of Cooking

Cooking for those I love enabled me to weave a new Mommy myth. Over the years, I've made more soup than I could possibly consume. Maternal instincts have grown beyond my children, extending to a family of friends. It's hormonally impossible for me to make small quantities. Nurturing others allows me to nurture myself. Pulling out my oversized soup pot gives me a thrill knowing the joy it brings. Each winter, my reputation as a loving cook grows; I'm no longer known for my past but for my healing chicken soup!

Hungry Mother Recipe: Chicken Soup

This versatile recipe can be adjusted for a clear broth by cutting the vegetables into larger chunks, for easy straining and removal after cooking. Or for a 'creamier' version, once fully cooked, puree the vegetables with an immersion blender in the same pot or place them in a food processor. I prefer to remove the chicken after cooked and put aside to add later.

Having chicken soup on hand in the freezer is worth its weight in gold. Many times arriving home from work, not feeling well or children have the sniffles, finding frozen stacks of 'gold bullion' in the freezer is a lifesaver. The trick to freezing soup is concentrated flavor and with that in mind, skip adding all the broth and water to keep the volume small; defrost and dilute with broth or water to your liking.

Ingredients

4-6 chicken thighs; bone-in/skin

1 large leek

1 large yellow onion, chopped

1 large leek, trimmed, washed well, medium-chopped

1 celery root [celeriac]; peeled, sliced, chopped or,
6 stalks, peel tough skin

2 large parsnips, peeled, sliced, or chopped

2 large carrots, peeled, sliced, or chopped

1 quart chicken broth or chicken bouillon cubes

fresh dill

sea salt

olive oil

grated ginger (optional)

4 cups water

Directions

1. In a large stockpot, add oil, heat over low flame. Add onion, leek until soft about 8-10 minutes.
2. Add chicken skin-side-down, let brown for 5-7 minutes, stirring to coat onion & leek. Remove chicken to plate, add the remaining vegetables. Let all the vegetables cook on medium heat, stirring so as not to burn or stick to the bottom of the pot for about 20 minutes, stirring occasionally.
3. Add water & chicken broth; if using bullion, dissolve first in ½ cup water, then add. Stir well. Add cooked chicken, cover, keep on low flame. Keep the dill in a bunch, place on top of the soup; do not stir in—it's an aromatic seasoning.
4. Cover and cook on low heat for 60 minutes. Taste the soup and season with salt.
5. Remove from heat and let sit until cool; remove chicken and the dill. Using a spoon, skim off any fat. For a clear broth, remove all vegetables and reserve for another use or discard. For a creamy texture, use an immersion blender and pulverize all the vegetables in the broth.
6. Add grated ginger and season to taste.
7. Add chicken (shredded, cut up, or whole) back in the soup. Serve hot.

Chapter 3

Making Amends
What's for Dinner

Memories are made in the kitchen. Coming home from school, sitting down in the kitchen, hearing the voice of the mother or father; the smell and taste create a visceral memory that stays with you your whole life. Cooking transcends feeding yourself; it is home, love, family, and security. Food memories are very powerful.

~Jacques Pepin, French-born American chef, author, and TV personality

Eating is one of life's certainties, and I used this to my advantage. Addiction had robbed my maternal instinct. In early recovery, cooking dinner on a daily basis was a passport back to my family. I ran our kitchen with heart and soul to make amends by showing my children I cared. Making a commitment to sobriety and tackling a new recipe takes a leap of faith. We gather the ingredients, follow the directions, and trust that the results will be delicious.

Cooking for my family, one meal at a time, improved the odds of staying sober. The ritual of making dinner structured my day, framing a graceful recovery. The ingredients for early sobriety include treatment, 12-step meetings, and a sober support community. The steps for making a meal require planning and preparation, plus a financial commitment. Setting money aside for necessities can be a challenge, as forgoing food for drugs is commonplace. There are no shortcuts or skipping corners as the results would be inedible. Making supper became a daily affirmation of my sobriety.

Recovery-focused behavioral mechanisms (repeated actions) lead to intermediate processes that enhance recovery stability and the progressive movement towards global health and social functioning. Such intermediate effects include increased hope for recovery, increased self-confidence in achieving recovery, improved decision-making and coping skills, increased family and social support, and spiritual awakening (sudden epiphanies and turning points; clarification of values and life goals; increased life meaning and purpose).

~William White, MSW addiction studies and author

In early recovery, there's an urgent need to change gears. It's the start of replacing a lifetime of bad habits and life-threatening pleasures. What better vehicle than the culinary experience to learn a healthy balance? Recovering people are starving for a life that matters, praying that it's more than just enduring as the odds of staying sober under those conditions are slim.

After fifteen years of sobriety, I fell behind codeine cough syrup. My husband had fallen in love with his next of several wives, and I found myself alone with an infant and toddler. Humiliation haunted me, not due to his infidelity but because of the business we built together, which now was off-limits. For a year, I used sleep medication to get through restless, tortured nights. Predictably, it progressed to codeine syrup after a bout of bronchitis, and finally, into a downward spiral for the next two years.

Lucky for me, I had accumulated a bank account of life-affirming interests from my earlier sobriety. I had a passion for all things culinary, and now, it was saving me. At four weeks sober, sobriety karma provided me an opportunity to host a new cooking segment, See Jane Cook, on cable TV. A few years earlier, the executive producer booked me as a recovery expert on a talk show. She was a personal friend and knew I was a great cook, at ease with feeding a crowd with homemade specialties and making it look easy.

Fresh out of detox, I could barely brush my teeth. Ironically, being more nervous about staying sober than how I appeared on camera put me at ease. Every week, an oversized limo chauffeured me to the studio, a boost to my forlorn Mommy image. My days were consumed with cooking, attending meetings, and reading food magazines and sobriety literature.

In early recovery, establishing a routine is a good thing, but at times I went overboard and overcooked, making elaborate meals as if a dozen dignitaries were coming to dinner. My girls begged only for tater tots and pizza bagels, but this sober mom was obsessed with replacing the nightmare of what I had become. What better place to start than the table? Our kitchen became the hub of our universe, where Mommy could be found chopping, mixing, or cleaning up.

My kids had front-row seats to my ugliest bottom. Chaos and uncertainty had ruled our roost. They were still uneasy from nearly two years of my strung-out and doped-up mood swings. At times, I'd disappear to the bedroom and hide under the sheets, stoned. It would take repeated gestures and time before they trusted my recovery. Cooking for them opened the door between us.

Once, a camera crew visited the house to film an episode in our kitchen. With flour flying and utensils scattered, each daughter demonstrated their specialty, smiling and confident. Years later, watching that CD I understood they were on a parallel journey, recovering beside me and from me. Acknowledging their emotions surrounding my recovery was essential for an honest relationship.

A simple, "What do you want for dinner?" granted them the right to recover their feelings. Their choices mattered to Mommy, sending a strong signal of unconditional love. Being sober, I took in my children's feelings without reacting, demonstrating adult behavior. Family activities were a priority, from shopping lists to supermarket safaris where we searched for ingredients. Together, we'd choose ripe fruits and vegetables or make substitutions, giving way to new concoctions, Paige's pasta, for example, and Teddie's turkey chili. At home, their little hands unpacked the groceries, putting them away in their rightful spots. Sometimes, they would help set the table or just play around me; other times, we worked together. Doing these tasks alone would take less time and effort, but I was determined to recruit and regain their confidence.

Reconnecting and rebuilding relationships is a slow-cooker process. "Progress, not perfection" and a dash of willingness are key. Making amends in small, significant ways anchored them to me. Shouting, "Dinner's ready!" soothed our house like a lullaby. Mealtime brought us together, even if just to bicker, a snapshot of normalcy. The routine of eating dinner together transformed the dining table into center stage for family drama. Similar to a hybrid support group, tears and fears boiled over without consequence. It was neutral territory, with no fuss, no muss, and plenty of paper towels. Early recovery is all about overwhelming feelings and then releasing them to reduce stress. Understanding that we shared this recovery connected us in loving ways.

Today, whatever is on the table is officially dinner and discovered there are no wrong answers in parenting. I have the authority to change my mind, the same as adding or subtracting an ingredient while cooking a pot roast and calling it my own. Soon, I learned a new confidence, not requiring any explanation.

"Because I said so. I'm your mother," can be my answer to anything.

*****

2006, Empty Nest

It was one of those unsettling dreams where I'd lost something really important, made worse by forgetting what it was. The plane's melodic lullaby lured me into a nap of complete disorientation. I was always easy prey for a catnap, as uninterrupted sleep had eluded me since 1983 when my oldest was born. Exhausted by one thousand errands, feet throbbing from unreasonable shoes on urban avenues, I awoke to the realization of leaving my youngest daughter one-time zone behind. The effort of ensconcing a freshman into dorm life and the reality of leaving her to manage everyday destiny in the Windy City washed over me. The sob fest began.

Maternal instincts are not always glamorous, as the weary businessman next to me could attest. Heaving, sobbing, eyes streaming, I began to take comfort in my open entitlement. I owned this festival of tears, and somehow it felt as right as pie. Motherhood should begin when it ends, but that day, my clarity felt as if it had arrived too late. Appreciation always gets a boost once you lose it. Didn't I know from the start that letting go was inevitable? Enviable? My job?

Through betrayal, divorce, and single parenthood, I raised two young daughters—one, coping with the challenges of juvenile diabetes, chronic absenteeism, and hard luck. The other, self-doubt, dysmorphia, and hopeless pursuit of Dad's approval. Today, both are fine, grown-up, lovely young women.

Over the years, I managed child support, paychecks, career changes, buying a home, making a home, and the accumulation of countless keepsakes in attics and basements. I was the ringmaster of birthday parties, playdates, sleepovers, sweet sixteens, and proms. The fearless leader in charge of locking up, power failures, and facing down menacing encounters. Mechanic to furnaces, blown fuses, flat tires, and overflowing toilets. Clinician to fevers, pimples, menstrual cramps, and a myriad of mysterious symptoms. Therapist for disappointments, playground brawls, and the endless doubts of puberty. Translator of the misguided antics of their father and his reluctance to behave like one. Tutor for homework, special projects, and math beyond comprehension. Solo participant at school performances, religious events, and late-night carpools. Navigator of SATs, college applications, financial aid, and moving them there. Moral Sherpa through honesty, respect, tolerance, envy, and defeat. Confidant to budding sexuality, lewd parties, and alcohol. Cheerleader to success, curiosity, and passions. And the icing on the cake, owning up to and sustaining my recovery alongside them in real time.

Bereft of my proudest accomplishment, motherhood defined my core element as the actualized person I had always hoped to become. My body of work as a mom activated the noblest part of my soul. "Mommy, Mommy," called out a hundred thousand times, awakened the sleeping giant of unconditional love. You can count on me always, every time, anywhere. You are my favorite people and I never tire of our relationship. Well, maybe while cranky from a menopausal spike, and sent to your rooms until you apologize. Belly to belly, growing cell into magical flesh, the sweetest nuzzle like no other. My daughters have started their own lives with hearts full, injected with the vaccine of total love. Intuitively and instinctively, loving themselves has grown into familiar terrain. My only regrets are linked to short-sightedness, short tempers, and lapses of maternal grace.

*****

Motherhood is an organic pleasure; your body and soul are innately tuned to your children's voices. Every baby is beautiful, our hands magnetized to tushies, nesting in their fragrant necks; every action they take is a wonder. I loved that part and feel lucky it all came so easily. My resolve was a reservoir of resources, the purest form of energy I had ever known. This vigor surprised me, as the motherlode of inner strength returned each morning after emotional bankruptcy the night before. Now, I was going home to vacant bedrooms and a silent kitchen. It's an oxymoron, home to nothing. Let me correct myself: one dog, three cats, rabbits, two Koi fish, the occasional stray, and a family of raccoons that are convinced my casa es su casa. But I was not going home empty. I was full to the brim with the achievement of raising my daughters to leave.

*****

Hungry Mother Tips

- "What do you want for dinner?" signals a message of unconditional love. Their choices matter to Mommy, granting them the right to recover their feelings.
- Reconnecting and rebuilding relationships is a slow-cooker process. "Progress, not perfection" with a dash of willingness is key. Making amends in small significant ways anchors children to us.
- Cooking for children opens the door between us. Calling out, "Dinner's ready," soothed our house like a lullaby

Benefit Of Cooking

What is considered tedious can be converted into a productive family activity; for example: washing, drying, and sorting basil leaves. Fresh basil is a source of fragrant joy in the summer months, and prepping it to make pesto sauce is best enjoyed outdoors.

It's reminiscent of a time when families harvested, canned, and stored fresh produce throughout the season. Pesto stores well in small amounts in the freezer or in a tightly closed jar in the refrigerator for several days. The best feature of this recipe is that you can add other ingredients that tickle your fancy at the vegetable stand or from your pantry. From tossing in cherry tomatoes or sundried tomatoes to substituting basil for kale and mint to using almonds instead of pignolia, every culture puts its own spin on fresh herbs and pasta—a golden opportunity for each family member to personalize and put their mark on a favorite recipe.

Hungry Mother Recipe: Pesto Sauce

Rinse off basil leaves in the sink, then place in a large bowl on a big table or use any flat surface available. Lay out a dish or some paper towels flat on the table. Taking one stem at a time, pull off leaves and place on a towel. Air dry well, then collect cleaned leaves, enough for four (4) cups.

Ingredients

4 cups fresh basil leaves

3-4 cloves garlic, peeled and crushed

Coarse salt (Kosher) and freshly ground pepper to taste

1/2 cup pignolia (pine) nuts

1/2 cup grated Parmesan cheese

1/4 cup tbsp grated Pecorino Romano cheese (optional)

1/2 cup olive oil

Directions

- Place garlic, pine nuts, and salt in a food processor with the motor running. Gradually add some of the oil in small amounts until blended.
- Add basil and, with the machine on, add some of the oil in a slow, steady stream.
- Again, with the motor running, add parmesan cheese with the remaining oil. Blend well.
- Spoon over warm pasta (your favorite) in a large bowl.

Tips: Toast nuts: Heat in a dry skillet over low heat until lightly golden and fragrant, remove and let cool. Watch closely—it can burn easily! Loosely pack washed basil leaves into a measuring cup. The pesto is dense and concentrated, with only a tablespoon or two needed for each serving of pasta. Each recipe yields about 2 cups of sauce.

Chapter 4

Acceptance
Kitchen Conversations With Myself

We need time to defuse, to contemplate. Just as in sleep our brains relax and give us dreams, so at some time in the day we need to disconnect, reconnect, and look around us.
~Laurie Colwin, author and food journalist

Sitting in cold basements on hard chairs, I learned to listen well. The benefits gained from attending thousands of meetings included cultivated patience and a chance to sort out feelings. Twelve-step meetings are a democratic process, and etiquette requires waiting your turn to share, a challenge for some. While waiting, my internal voice ran rampant, from blaming others to rationalizing addictive behavior to wallowing in self-pity. After months of ranting and raving to myself, even I grew tired of my own complaints and was ready for a new dialogue.

Beginners' meetings have a tension all their own. At ninety days, you're expected to qualify and share your story of how you earned a seat in the rooms. Embarrassed, because this was my second time around, I chose a homegroup out of my neighborhood, driving the short distance to the Upper West Side of Manhattan. Next door to Lincoln Center and ABC, it was filled with actors, filmmakers, musicians, and artists, an intimidating audience. Ninety days were approaching, and I was filled with fear and a less-than-zero ego, obsessing over my qualification. Rehearsing in the car or while showering or making dinner, I realized that verbalizing thoughts out loud gave murky emotions shape and perspective.

Like ketchup or salt, anger and hurt are condiments to early recovery. I had a laundry list of resentments for nearly everyone and everything and indulged in imaginary confrontations while cooking. Talking to myself opened the door to telling off all the people who angered me and gave me a chance to sort out daily dilemmas. I granted myself the freedom to curse and accuse; after all, it's my kitchen, my court—no arguments! Standing by the stove, big spoon in hand, most resentments sounded ludicrous, and I tossed them out like moldy bread. Those kitchen conversations offered relief and release, similar to attending a meeting, calling a sponsor, or reading literature. It was a proactive experience of self-preservation, a way to reconnect with my internal compass and resilient nature.

While I was pregnant with our youngest daughter, their dad fell in love with his second, soon-to-be ex-wife. My children were obligated to visit him every other weekend and on holidays, with a new stepmom ready and waiting to pamper and coo. They celebrated Thanksgiving, birthdays, and the tooth fairy, all without me. Returning home with new hairstyles, shiny barrettes, and painted nails, I was fit to be tied. On alternating Fridays and Sundays, the children switched locations, lifestyles, and rules. Sunday-night transitions inevitably morphed into Monday madness.

Getting dropped, swapped, and strapped into car seats amplified their feelings of confusion. Meal and bedtime routines were abandoned while they were away from home, and they returned to me hyperactive, overstimulated, and sleep-deprived. Those Sunday nights became a hellish ritual as well-behaved children transformed into fussy aliens from another universe. The journey from our house to his and home again was reminiscent of a Chinese fire drill. As they grew older, Freudian issues and puberty made it worse. I walked on eggshells most Monday mornings with a fifty/fifty chance that by dinner, feelings could cascade into chaos and tantrums.

Friends and therapists warned me to put my feelings aside and accept the positive aspects, patiently reassuring me that no one could take my place. Relinquishing my daughters' care to the woman who broke up my marriage was not an easy pill to swallow. Rage, lust for revenge, and resentment naturally take over. That seething anger had the potential to push me to the edge of giving up and picking up. In time, those quiet conversations with myself and others taught me acceptance. The real world presents disappointments and unfair realities. Embracing acceptance makes it easier to navigate life on life's terms. Stirring a delicious sauce on the stove makes this harsh fact sweeter to swallow.

Facing character defects taught me how to decipher my children's complaints and dramatic outbursts, and I soon realized that usually, it was not about me. I became an expert at emotional dumpster diving, sifting through what was valid and what to toss out. My daughters, still hesitant about my sobriety, often masked their true feelings, and I had to remember, it was their drama, not mine. Knowing this made their outbursts easier for me to manage and not overreact to. Addicts are not good at hearing criticism. We cannot afford to listen—it threatens our agenda. Learning to pause and listen before responding made me a better mother. The art of listening is a valuable, emotional tool.

*****

1998, Sunday-Night Transition Blues

It was a Monday night dinner after my youngest spent the weekend with Dad. Her demeanor was stiff, and I was thoughtful about supper for this very reason, making roasted chicken with baby potatoes.

Daughter: "I hate this chicken. Why can't you make it a different way?" she asked, contorting her face into an expression that could stop a clock.

Mom: "I always make it this way. Then just eat the potatoes."

Daughter: "Yeah, well, I hate the potatoes too. They're disgusting and gross. I'm not hungry anyway. Can I leave the table?"

Mom: "We just sat down, and I haven't seen you all weekend. Anything happen in school today?" Pre-teen body language betrayed her, all tangled and tight, eyes staring down at the table. It was not anger; it was pain and disappointment.

Silly me. It was the transition blues. Hate my cooking? Gee, nasty insult. Big feelings had to be going on. I swallowed a painful jab to the essence of my motherhood, but as the adult here, I refused to be pulled down that rabbit hole. I waited a few seconds before responding, mentally rewinding the past days' events.

Mom: "Ah, well" (trying to stall and pump for information). "Did you have a fight with Brianna?"

Daughter: "Mom, why do you always think I've had a fight just because I'm not hungry and hate your cooking? You always ask the same stupid questions. No, nothing happened today, and if it did, you wouldn't understand."

Mom: "Did you have fun with Daddy?" Bingo! Her gorgeous hazel eyes grew huge and moist as paintbrush lashes furiously blinked to hold back a dump truck of tears. "Did you go to the movies?"

Daughter: Her response barely a whisper, "Yeah, it was okay."

Mom: "Where did you have dinner afterward? Did you go to a restaurant?"

Daughter: "Daddy made a barbecue at the beach house."

Mom: "Oh, was it good? What did he make?"

Daughter: "Chicken. It was the best chicken I ever ate, and I wish I had some now!"

There was the reason for her complaints about my "horrible" chicken, but it wasn't like their dad to cook just for the kids, something single moms did every night of their lives. It must have been a special occasion.

Mom: "Did Daddy have company? Anyone else come over for dinner?" Silence. The tempo of our conversation had skipped some significant beats. "Sweetie, were Grandma and Grandpa there?"

No answer. I figured it must be serious as my daughter was never at a loss for words. "Did Dad have a date?" An oxymoron. How could a daddy have a date if not with your mommy?

To make a long, tiring story short, their dad had repeated history by cheating on their lovely second mom after a few years of marriage. My kids were devastated, and even though I took secret delight in the universal scheme of karmic payback, I was truly disappointed. Weekend visitation, once a well-oiled piece of machinery, fell apart. Plans and any semblance of continuity were ruined. The girls had been exposed to the carcass of another disintegrating marriage with a side order of expired explanations.

Daughter: "Yeah, her name is Natasha."

Her demeanor reflected what wives had encapsulated and packaged so well, the other woman. Standing up with feet firmly planted on the kitchen floor, she shot me an expression of loss way past her years, a betrayed woman. Okay, Mom, tread lightly. This is your daughter's nightmare, not yours.

I carefully measured my words as I explained this to their dad on the phone. "You only see them every other weekend, once every fourteen days. Do you think it's possible to restrain yourself and not bring a date? These are the golden years of childhood. You have two lovely daughters. Isn't that enough company for you?"

Knowing where this conversation was headed, it was his loss as the girls became less inclined to participate in weekend visits. Yet I remained ever watchful for the necessary slice of "Love Pie," always encouraging and arranging their time to ensure a relationship with their dad despite my personal feelings on the subject.

Sometimes bad pie is better than no pie at all.

*****

The ritual of food preparation offers a quiet time for contemplation, a sanctuary for thought. Our lives are complicated with many side issues. By giving pause to untangle events, we can figure things out. Cooking calms me and washing, peeling, and chopping vegetables allows the mind to drift. Preoccupation with multi-tasking clears an emotional space, free-floating and unencumbered. Feelings come into focus, and others fade into the background, creating a state called culinary meditation.

My children needed a full portion of love, but I could not master the parenting universe alone. With emotional resources already stretched, I came to believe in the Love Pie for extra slices of love. Whether they get two slices from me, or one from Dad, neighbors, playmates' parents, or grandparents, it serves up a full portion of caring and security.

Our circle of friends took us under their wings, inviting us to holiday dinners, Sunday barbecues, and family vacations. I didn't bake the pie, but I organized it by gathering the ingredients from family and friends, remaining ever vigilant for potential slices. The Love Pie became a blessing in disguise as my daughters are astonishingly agile at reaching out to different people. They've cultivated a family of friends with strong, significant bonds at times more responsive than relatives. An essential relationship skill, it is a life preserver against drowning. If one relationship fails, they intuitively grab outstretched hands to be pulled into the safety of an available lifeboat.

*****

Hungry Mother Tips

- This is not the Spanish Inquisition. Don't pump your kids for information. Eventually, you'll hear about the good, the bad, and the ugly.
- Refrain from judging your kid's feelings. It's one of the few things that truly belong to them. Their reactions,

especially after visitation, reflect core conflicts and emotional fall-out from your divorce. File for later discussion after calm has prevailed.

- Your ex is somebody's father; keep your opinions to yourself. Once something is said, it's hard to take back.

Benefit Of Cooking

Everyone loves making pie and this recipe calls for little hands to help blend butter into flour, producing crust and indelible memory. Making pie is not an easy or casual task; it requires diligence, patience, and a dash of grit, all the ingredients necessary to solidify relationships. Conversations while making pie tend to be meaningful, offering a chance to verbalize deep feelings. When completed, we stand back and admire our efforts, amazed at how it all came together, as a family.

Hunger Mother Recipe: Love Pie Galette

The filling can be made with any seasonal fruit, from peaches to berries. In the winter, try savory vegetables by adding grated cheese to the crust. My favorite is Gruyère cheese with caramelized onions as the filling, reminiscent of French onion soup. Using this crust recipe, we can fill it up with anything on hand while being mindful of ingredients for the next. A Love Pie always satisfies, no matter the filling.

Crust

2 cups all-purpose flour, plus more for dusting

1 cup almond flour (not almond meal)

2 sticks (16 oz.) very cold unsalted butter*

1/2 cup cold plain whole yogurt (not Greek)

1 tbsp ice-cold water, plus up to 3 tbsp more, if needed

1 tsp granulated sugar, plus more for sprinkling

1/2 tsp kosher salt

Egg wash: 1 egg beaten with 1 tsp yogurt or water

Filling

1/2 to 3/4 cup granulated sugar

1/2 tsp finely grated lemon zest

5 cups fresh strawberries hulled and halved

3 tbsp arrowroot or cornstarch

Small pinch of salt. *If using salted butter, omit

Directions

1. Whisk both flours with 1 tsp sugar and salt in a large bowl.
2. Cut butter into 1/2-inch cubes and spread over flour. Using pastry blender or your fingers, blend butter into flour mixture until chunks are pea-size. This takes effort and energy; assign a child to complete this task.
3. Drizzle the yogurt over the flour and butter mixture. Use a wooden spoon/spatula to toss and combine. If the dough seems dry, drizzle 1 tbsp ice water and continue tossing and combining, incorporating any dry flour at bottom of the bowl until the mixture comes together in a mound. If needed, drizzle more ice water, 1 tbsp at a time, making sure not too wet.
4. Transfer dough to a large piece of plastic wrap, press dough into a 6-inch disk, and wrap well. Refrigerate for at least 2 hours or up to 3 days.
5. Heat oven to 400 degrees with the rack in the center position. Line a sheet pan with parchment paper.
6. Make egg wash: Whisk in a small bowl/measuring cup by adding 1 tbsp water; set aside.

Filling: Place ½ cup sugar and lemon juice in a large bowl; blend into the sugar with your fingertips. Add the strawberries, arrowroot/cornstarch, and salt; mix well to combine. Add up to another ¼ cup sugar to taste, depending on the sweetness of your strawberries and your desired level of sweetness.

Crust: Dust countertop with flour and place chilled dough on it; sprinkle a little flour on top of the dough. Continually dust the rolling pin with flour as well. Roll dough out to a 12- to 14-inch round, lightly flouring as needed. (It's okay if the edges break and the shape isn't perfectly round.) Gently transfer the dough by using a flat spatula, and place onto the prepared baking sheet. If you have to pause, place dough in fridge to keep chilled.

Pile the strawberries and their juices in the middle of the dough, leaving a 2-inch border. Fold the border over the fruit, pleating as you fold and leaving the center of the galette exposed. Brush the crust with the egg wash and sprinkle with sugar. Bake until the crust is golden and the strawberries are bubbling for about 35 minutes. The crust should appear goldened. If the galette is stuck in pan, cut around parchment paper and remove to cool on a wire rack for 1 hour and serve.

Chapter 5

Recover Authority
Your Place at the Table

A home-cooked meal is a source of joy for audience and chef alike. It's more than the sum of its parts, where blending chopped meat, egg, Worcestershire sauce and breadcrumbs magically becomes meatloaf. Supper symbolizes a communal evening meal, the pleasures of a stable family. It's as close as we get to the old-fashioned virtue of the good mother who stays home always available when family needs us. It's a homey paradise of childhood where we share easily and listen seriously.

~Nora Ephron, American journalist, author, and filmmaker

Admitting addiction to the children we parent is a watershed, life-changing moment. It's motherhood in real-time where ego, our past, and the woman we hope to be, converge. It puts into clear focus what it means to be a sober mom; honesty about our "recovery reality" shapes our behavior and allocates credit for sustaining sobriety. Parenting newly sober generates a lot of stress. Decisions that seem callous and uncaring to those around us are, in truth, putting our desire to stay straight first. Sobriety is selfish and understanding the dynamics can help reduce the tension of asserting your authority.

Anyone who has tried to get sober understands it is not easy, and for sober moms, it takes double the effort of regular people. We work our program while caring for children and managing family life, as most are single moms. The 12-step program asks us to commit without the guilt of paying less attention to other aspects of our lives. Not so for mothers, with no days off from parenting or our 12-step program. We don't have the luxury of putting children on hold until we're on more solid sobriety ground. The physical, emotional, and spiritual challenges of recovery can eat up every ounce of energy. With plenty of overtime.

*****

1994, Silver Hill

I should have sold our house as soon as the divorce became final, but it took five years of insanity before I could admit life had become unmanageable. The original snapshot of what I expected my life to look like was shattered, and now I was obsessed with staying in our house and community. We don't need any daddy. We'll make it on our own. I'll zap my career into overdrive and earn enough to stay. Divorce shouldn't mean we can't afford our original life! The reality was shameful enough; I couldn't admit defeat and leave like a dog with my tail dragging behind.

Wrong answer! What the hell was I thinking? This was classic addictive thinking, operating from a ruptured state of mind. All the emotional growth I achieved from fifteen years of sobriety flew out the window. Imagine a storybook illustration—a woman at the helm of a boat, in rough seas, hair flying wild while the crew, all under the age of five, watch in horror. Still, it was no excuse, having fought tooth and nail ten years earlier to get sober. I knew better but was feeling increasingly worse. Heading home from work, exhausted from my own day, then greeted at the door with the demanding enthusiasm that young children save for parents...

"Watch me, watch me, Mommy." A Greek chorus for attention. "You promised we could bake tonight for my birthday party at school." My youngest tugged at my arm, physically trying to jar the memory of a weary agreement. "Mommy, Mommy, hurry up," my oldest daughter asserted anxiously. "We're late for my dance recital. Did you buy the white tights I need?" Suspicion in her voice. "Oh, no, you forgot.

Oh, Mommy, I need them for tonight. If we leave now, we can stop at the store on our way there."

I had the sensation of eyeballs fluttering up to the ceiling, appealing to a higher power for strength and inspiration. Screw that! I craved physical relief and knew swallowing a pill would be instant and easier. Coat still on, I was tapped out and French-fried, only wanting to go upstairs, rip off my work clothes, and lie prone for twenty minutes. But my kids had not seen me since eight a.m., and they were needy too. Feeling like a soul survivor, the sole provider of emotional security and unconditional love was stretching my resolve till it snapped.

It started innocently enough with a sympathetic (lecherous is more accurate, but that's another story) psychiatrist prescribing a mild sedative for sleepless nights. Truth be told, I was fearful locking up every night, listening with one ear for sounds that went bump in the dark, and the other ear on the hormonal radar system, tracking the coughs and whimpers of young children. Honestly, I hadn't had a sound night's sleep since their dad left, and like a prisoner subjected to sleep deprivation, my resistance shriveled.

My intellect lectured what I knew so well: Substances cannot solve or change the problem. That only certainty was crashing into the proverbial brick wall. Once an addict, always an addict; my gut did not give a damn as I craved relief. My metabolism welcomed the barbiturate derivative with open arms as nerve syntaxes quickly skyrocketed past old tolerances. It wasn't long before one pill turned into two. A few months later, diagnosed with nasty bronchitis and a hacking cough, a prescribed dose of codeine cough syrup delivered the soundest sleep since my ex left.

Hooked again, that obscure, soothing cherry-flavored elixir was my nirvana. I couldn't help but think, *Isn't it ironic,* Alana (Alana Morrisette, "Ironic", Jagged Little Pill, 1996) the narcotic responsible for my current demise was prescribed at age nine for asthma? I fell in love with that feeling, spending my entire drug career trying to duplicate that first free-fall nod and stupor. It's true—we spend our lives trying to recapture all the firsts that scratch indelible ink on our soul—first love, first kiss...

That's how I ended up at Silver Hill in 1994, after being clean and sober for nearly fifteen years. Its country club facade set deep in the woods of Connecticut looked like my final frontier. Nothing prepared me for the complete humiliation of another psychiatric hospitalization. Despite personal wisdom and my expertise in substance abuse, I ignored all the red flags, including the dents in my car, piles of unopened mail, and the dozen empty bottles of cough syrup hidden under my bathroom sink. It was only through the fear of losing custody that my brain recognized the brick wall I had slammed into.

My reality is simple. I have an addictive personality, not with people, places, and things, just narcotics. My metabolism has a photographic memory; it carries around a snapshot from 1976, the last time I shot dope. Watching *Trainspotting* two decades later, the little hairs on the back of my neck got stiff, and I swear, I could smell Mexican Mud cooking up in a spoon wafting out of the TV.

During the 1970s, while some were expanding their spiritual horizons in India or by communal living in isolated locations, I was on a pharmacological safari searching for the ultimate out-of-body experience. No drug was too expensive or dangerous as I scaled the mountains and valleys of death-defying episodes to achieve nirvana. By 1976, after five psychiatric hospitalizations, I entered AREBA, a therapeutic community, and lived there for one year, where I would finally recover and reclaim my life.

*****

Back in the parenting saddle sober, profound guilt from my substance abuse made it impossible to discipline. I carried around double guilt, first from neglecting my children while getting high and now from placing their needs seemingly second, behind my sobriety. It became an insidious cycle; constantly acquiescing to my children and doubting my decisions as it became harder and harder to be strict. I would clean their rooms, not enforce chores, and buy gifts impulsively. Rational choices don't spring from guilt, and guilt was overshadowing my erratic discipline. I had to break the cycle of parenting from a place of low esteem and take the risk that my decisions were right. It was time to get over the guilt.

My children lost patience with me, loudly protesting or quietly hurt whenever my sobriety took priority over their needs. Getting through the day drug-free ate up most of my energy, leaving me desperate for a second wind especially late afternoon, always a trigger point. Fighting the urge to use, maintaining employment, picking up the kids, making dinner, then finding an hour for a meeting or my own time-out was essential to carve out some serenity. Getting sober is selfish; it involves putting the goal of getting better for ourselves first and then for the people we love. It's the same instructions for an airplane emergency—adults are instructed to use the oxygen mask first, then on the children.

There's a temptation to make up for time lost by baking brightly colored sprinkled cupcakes, a fantasy I had to lose. The addictive traits of avoiding confrontation were mirrored in my parenting; it was all about appeasing and soothing. While active, my discipline was all over the place; it was random and unreasonable, and I lacked confidence in my parenting skills.

At first, when claiming some personal time and space, my children would throw my program back at me or whine that we never did or went to places they want. All my "free" time was for meetings, phone calls, or taking care of the house. Hesitating for a moment, old feelings of inadequacy settled over me. Still plagued by low self-esteem, it felt impossible to get back parental control and be a mother in charge.

Each day, little by little, recovery empowered me, and I declared myself redeemed. By communicating the truth and sharing feelings, children begin to understand that sobriety is for the greater good of the family. Over time, seeing all my efforts to make things better ultimately earned their respect.

Restoring authority is key to parenting. Without it, all hell can break loose, increasing the chances of a relapse. What helped me re-establish authority was to pause before responding. Children always want Mommy's attention and affection, with each age group demanding it in different ways. From bedtime stories to driving places to the dozen daily requests and complaints, my parenting resolve was constantly tested. "Mommy," "Mommy," "Mommy," called out one hundred times a day, challenged my patience and sobriety. I claimed my parental right by not answering immediately, giving myself a moment to catch my breath and think things over. What a concept! The compulsion for quick answers subsided because I wasn't lying anymore.

Honesty in recovery eliminates the need to think of a suitable answer, and I was no longer tossing out remarks or threatening consequences unable to sustain. I gave myself the luxury of contemplating an answer by not responding right away and then calling a friend or peer for feedback, all of which increased the chances of a positive outcome. Soon I learned that there are no right or wrong answers in parenting, just better ones.

Juggling all the responsibilities and roles without losing sight of sobriety took vigilance and energy beyond expectation. All I could do was my best each day. Taking personal inventory late at night, recounting all the effort and tasks accomplished, I was able to bestow credit on myself as a conscious parent. That confidence grew each day, making it easier to stand firm in my decisions and eventually allowing me to reply, "Because I am the mother," and soon realized that could be my answer to anything. The blood, sweat, and tears to become a sober mom granted me the right to demand respect. No longer a doormat to addiction, I was ready to reclaim my seat at the head of the table. I'd earned it.

I shared my sober reality and was proud of it. Raising my daughters as a single, sober mom was a blessing in disguise, and eventually, they appreciated and were proud of my journey. Falling from grace played back as a cautionary tale; no matter how low a fall, you can always get back up. The wisdom of understanding consequences before shit happens is a valuable insight growing up. Becoming sober served as a model of perseverance and strength in the face of major obstacles. Over time, my children came to admire how I pulled myself out of a difficult situation and thrived.

*****

Hungry Mother Tips

- Rational choices don't spring from guilt. Parent from a place of self-esteem. You're sober now. Leave the guilt behind.
- Pause before responding and claim your parental rights. Children are not your boss; they can wait for an answer. Give yourself time to consider your options; call another parent, a friend, or sponsor.
- Recovery empowers, redeems, and ultimately restores respect. Reclaim your seat at the head of the table, as you are no longer someone who is a doormat to addiction. You've earned it.
- In parenting, there are no right or wrong answers, just better ones.

It's important to be victorious in areas we can control. The last-minute panic of "Oh my gosh, what's for dinner tonight?" unprepared, unnerved, and unforgiving, can undermine sobriety. It's essential to set ourselves up for success, and putting dinner together is a great way to pat ourselves on the back and please everyone's tummy.

Benefit Of Cooking

Family life happens in the sanctuary of the kitchen. It's where we get to reassure children everything will be okay and allay their fears. Making supper became a daily affirmation of my sobriety and a chance to earn my place back at the table, present and in charge. The act of meal preparation made me an authority on dinner, and if you want to eat, you needed to respect that.

Hungry Mother Recipe: Gazpacho

Looking for a good way to show you mean business? Then it's time to pulverize some vegetables! Show your strength by smooshing ingredients into smithereens. Making gazpacho is an exercise in instincts and good judgment as you choose tomatoes and peppers on the spot by their looks and estimate how much they will yield. There are as many recipes for gazpacho as there are different types of tomatoes; make it your own. Taking a bunch of unruly, unrelated vegetables and blending them to make a refreshing summer soup is magical. Amaze children, friends, and yourself!

Ingredients

1 small red onion, peeled and roughly cut into chunks

1 large green pepper; scrape out seeds and white pulp, cut into chunks

1 cubanelle pepper; scrape out seeds and white pulp, cut into chunks

1-2 cloves garlic

3-4 celery stalks (optional); wash, trim, cut into chunks

1 cucumber; peel, scoop out seeds, cut into chunks

3 large ripe tomatoes, yellow or red (not plum); cut and scrape out excess seeds, cut into chunks

1/3 - 1/2 cup extra-virgin olive oil, more to taste, plus more for drizzling

3-4 tbsp red or sherry vinegar, more to taste

1-2 tsp Dijon mustard

Salt to taste

Directions

1. The gazpacho should have a semi-chunky consistency. As the food processor is running entire process, it can reduce the tomatoes to a watery pulp if first in. Start with onions, peppers, celery, garlic.
2. Place and pulse in a food processor or blender until chunky; you can add a bit of oil for easier blending.
3. Add tomato and cucumber; work in batches if needed.
4. Use high speed and pulse until blended but slightly chunky, pausing occasionally to scrape down the sides with a rubber spatula.
5. With the motor running, add the vinegar, oil, and mustard. The mixture will turn bright orange or dark pink and become smooth and emulsified, like a salad dressing. If it still seems watery, add more olive oil; if too thick add cold water, until the texture is creamy.
6. Chill before serving.

Chapter 6

Instincts & Intuition

Make Any Recipe Your Own

...satisfying man's hunger for food is not a matter of nutrition alone, but of satisfying his appetite for meaning, for values, for quality in the way he lives his life each day.
~Maguelonne Toussaint-Samat, French author, *A History of Food*

My internal compass was broken. As an addict, I had lost the difference between right and wrong. I was going in the opposite direction from everything that mattered, risking it all just to get high. Strung out, my best relationships were with drugs and the people I got them from. Only street smarts mattered, and I took a strange pride in being tough, the furthest from who I was. Rationalization ruled healthy intuition, and instincts were non-existent.

At first, I thought being sober was enough, but after a few months, I realized the quality of my relationships was lacking. Now, I wanted more. Embarrassed and ashamed from falling after fifteen years of sobriety, my low self-esteem kept me from bonding with others. I was at a crossroads. Regaining instincts and intuition in recovery starts when we begin to trust our peers and their judgment. Attending 12-step meetings offered a reality check, a framework for rational thinking, gained from listening to others. Sharing feelings was a way to put a voice to my emotions out in the open and get constructive feedback. I worked at cultivating a peer group and sponsor whose opinions and philosophy made sense, ultimately forming friendships that bonded us. Restoring instincts and intuition does not happen in a vacuum; it comes from the feedback of people we trust.

*****

1988, Trust your gut

My overstretched belly vibrated with this shriek-fest putting me into labor. The fear of childbirth was diminished by heartbreak, the perfect foil for pain. We had been fighting since two a.m. when he walked in, disheveled, with a half-baked excuse. We made a truce long enough to drop our four-year-old daughter at nursery school and then speed down the West Side Highway during rush hour to Mt. Sinai Hospital. While driving, his adrenaline shifted into high gear, and losing patience with traffic, he exited off in Harlem. Navigating streets circa The French Connection, he caught the attention of a policeman who promptly pulled us over. "Officer, my-wife-is-having-a-baby," he uttered (every husband's golden ticket), which was followed by the cop's effervescent, "Okay-folks-let's-boogie-follow-me," and we proceeded to race down 5th Avenue to 98th Street and into a parking spot by the front door. Unheard of luck!

My quick labor had my husband riveted, but once finished, he turned obnoxious, demanding a room for me immediately, saying he had to leave. Last night's events flashed back with an unspeakable premonition—he was desperate to be somewhere else, with someone else. Our baby girl was perfect but of no interest to him.

I was moved into a private room, given a small dose of pain medication, and fell into a deep sleep. The next morning, I called our house to remind him to bring my suitcase, which was left behind in the rush. The babysitter fumbled over the phone. "Oh, gee, um, he didn't sleep here last night. Isn't he there with you?" Then I calmly dialed the office. His secretary, never at a loss for words, stammered, "Oh, gee, um, he's not here. Isn't he with you?" Where the fuck is he? I wondered. Months of denials and absurd excuses gelled in a moment of clarity. He's having an affair. To be accurate, he'd fallen in love with the second of four future wives.

The afterglow of childbirth, that sunny February overlooking Central Park, was glorious in an unexpectedly sobering way. With newborn suckling at my breast, alone on the maternity floor, twelve years of sobriety paid off in a flood of self-esteem. In that sacred moment, I connected the dots of our fights, his attitude, and my feelings of neglect. Deep within, I understood things had to change, and because I was sober, anything was possible. Motherhood empowered my sobriety, and I believed the three of us deserved better.

My internal compass worked again, no more numbing self-doubt. If it smells like rotting fish, it is. Sobriety grants back instincts, and—my gut feelings were right-on.

That narcissist had tricked me and made our infant and toddler victims of his indiscretions. I vowed that day to hire a private investigator so I could file for divorce with confidence. Eventually, I obtained proof that he had gone off the deep end as a sex addict and intuitively knew that no amount of rehab could fix him. I had to end our marriage.

*****

Active addiction numbs us to everything and everyone, making it impossible to identify emotions. In early abstinence, after years of brushing feelings aside, the highs and lows rise to the surface, and something begins to stir physically in our stomach. That gut feeling signals the return of instincts that need to be practiced and nourished. Intuition comes from the innate ability to survive—we're born with it, those gut feelings that have served mankind throughout time. Motherhood is a driving force to get sober, and I made a conscious effort to tap into that energy. The nightly ritual of tucking my girls into bed became a touchstone, an evening affirmation of sobriety. That quiet time of the day allowed my thoughts to slow down and speak in a maternal voice; my mother's intuition was restored. Confidence in my instincts allowed responsible parenting to flow naturally with much less effort.

Decision-making as a single mom was a solo act. Life happened at the speed of light. It was critical to trust my instincts; otherwise, I'd be second-guessing every decision. High anxiety and self-doubt would surely follow, a set-up for a slip that had to be nipped in the bud. Reconnecting with our inner voice takes practice and meditation, which is why cooking works so well for me. Being in the kitchen, cleaning up, planning a meal, or shopping for ingredients grants quiet contemplation. Kitchen activities clear a personal space, a retreat from the daily chaos, a moment to pause and reflect—culinary meditation. In recovery, feelings can accumulate to a boiling point, and just like a pressure cooker letting off steam, it is part of the process. Dealing with overwhelming stress by making a favorite recipe is a pleasant, productive way to decrease anxiety and form a deeper connection to a healthy intuition. And makes everyone's tummy happy.

Substance abuse makes good parenting impossible—they're mutually exclusive. From front-row seats, my young daughters watched the mommy they loved slowly disappear. Instinctively, they pulled back. Something in their gut signaled all was not right. Newly sober, my heart ached to repair our relationship. On weekend nights, I stayed home to pay off the debt of subjecting them to my relapse, a choice that translated into a sobriety safety net to catch me from falling. Over time, my daughters gained confidence in my recovery, making me an easy mark for inviting their friends over; I rarely turned down requests. I took comfort and pride in seeing a crowd of adolescents in our house; even their stomping in and out brought satisfaction despite the chaos. It was a chance to meet my daughters' friends, feed them, and size up the troublemakers and sweethearts—pure proactive parenting.

As a sober mom, I wasn't asleep at the wheel, and if my girls acted out, I'd find out. After all, it was their fears and the power of peer pressure that drove them to behave badly. Today, my credibility with my daughters is a treasure that keeps me on my sober toes.

Getting close to others is a stepping stone to restoring instincts and intuition, a life-changing event. I gained confidence in my instincts and maturity with all types of acquaintances. Eventually, close, meaningful relationships became one of the greatest reasons to stay sober. Without them, it's unlikely I'd stay clean. Over time, trusting instincts enabled me to follow my passions and live the life that I was truly meant to live. I've embraced the things that fill me with joy and passion: trying new activities and expanding my horizons. From sailing to making a meal for a mob to meditating in the quiet calm of nature—I'm constantly securing the life I hoped for in recovery.

*****

Hungry Mother Tips

- When it comes to children, your instincts are correct.
- Body language is an open book; learn to read. From face muscles to a lighter tread on the stairs, you know this dance. Watch for changes in the choreography.
- When traditional comforts, hobbies, or friends are abandoned, check it out. Ten to one, your kid has a partner in crime; never be embarrassed to call around and find out.
- If it's too good to be true, it probably is.

Benefit Of Cooking

Good cooks trust their instincts. The food experience is deeply rooted within us, whether realized or not. It just takes a little guidance and faith in our senses to know when an egg is done or if that fish needs flipping or if the soup needs salt. Whether adding a pinch or lowering the flame, we intuitively know what to do next.

Instinct is not a destination but a path, moving us toward the answer. This is true for cooking and sobriety. We are all chefs with our best interests at heart and only need to find our creative selves to take the plunge, with or without a recipe. Over time, we develop intelligence in our fingertips by touching the food we cook—does it feel ripe or smell fresh? That's culinary instinct! All it takes is concentration on the task at hand; trust yourself and go for it.

Hungry Mother Recipe: Nanny's BBQ Chicken

My fondest childhood memory starts with Nanny's barbequed chicken, best cooked on an outdoor grill. My grandfather hand-built the brick fireplace, using a thick steel plate as the grill, and sweated with a smile for hours while he hand-turned each piece. Guests inevitably took turns standing by him while he cooked; it seemed each one had a story, a confidence to tell. It was my proud responsibility to tend the fire by his side, adding paper or wood scrapes intuitively as needed, and bring him cool drinks, which he gulped down. I still have all those barbeque tools, his initials carved into the wood handles, and use them to this day. Over time, family recipes are rarely precise, as each one puts on a personal twist. All it takes is tasting at every stage and if it sparks a memory of a meal, favorite flavor, or a time of year, you've nailed it.

For best results, partially (par) bake chicken in the oven first, then grill. I always make extra portions as it's delicious cold the next day after marinating overnight in the same cooked sauce.

Ingredients

10-12 pieces cut-up chicken (I prefer breasts and thighs); rinse well; a little wet when ready to cook is okay.

1 bottle Heinz chili ketchup

1 large can puree or crushed tomatoes

1 small can tomato paste

1/2 cup brown sugar

1/4 cup molasses

2-3 tbsp apple cider vinegar

2 tbsp French mustard or dry mustard

2 tbsp canola oil

Grate: 4-5 cloves garlic, 2 tbsp ginger (optional)

2 tbsp smoked (Spanish) paprika

1 tsp salt

1/4 tsp Cayenne pepper (optional)

Directions

1. Add all ingredients, except chicken, into a large bowl, big enough to hold all the chicken. Blend well and taste. Feel free to add more vinegar, molasses, brown sugar, mustard, and spices. Make it your own!
2. Add chicken to sauce and marinate for several hours; overnight is ideal but not necessary.
3. Preheat oven to 400 degrees; bake for 30-40 minutes.
4. Pour everything into a large baking pan with chicken in a single layer; line with tin foil to avoid messy clean-up.
5. Warm up the grill and spray with Pam to coat. Once heated up, "stab" a piece of chicken; let excess sauce drip back into the baking pan.

NOTE: if the chicken is too "wet" with sauce, it will drip onto the grill and possibly extinguish the flame—very messy. Hold each piece over the bowl and let excess fall off. Place biggest pieces on first, skin-side-up (breasts take 10 minutes longer), then add the remainder. Grill approximately 10 minutes, then turn over to skin side. Cook another 5-10 minutes, watching carefully as skin is delicate and can stick. Check continuously as each grill is different; “char” without burning. Remove chicken as done and place back into the pan of cooked sauce; let sit for a few minutes, turning to coat each piece. Serve warm. Include some hearty bread to soak up sauce or drizzle over cooked rice.

Chapter 7

Life-Affirming Activities
Find a Passion

Cooking is at once child's play and adult joy.
And cooking done with care is an act of love.
~Craig Claiborne, food critic

Finding drugs, getting drugs, the excitement of it all, used to thrill me. It was part of the package, taking risks and surviving, a danger junkie. In the end, with no friends, drugs were my only way to bond with people. The camaraderie with other addicts is forged against the background hum of illegal activity, gluing us together. I missed that instant connection desperately when I was first sober. Quality of life is not possible strung out and searching for that passion is awkward at first. Substance abuse kept me apart and isolated, just the way I liked it. The biggest challenge of recovery was losing that cranky junkie attitude, forcing me out of my shell. My fondest memories of marriage were on our sailboat, a twenty-three-foot Ensign designed for handling rough seas. Working side by side in the boatyard, spring and fall gave way to summer sunset sails and afternoon adventures. I was at my happiest learning to navigate, manage the sails, or prepare for an approaching storm, challenged yet in control.

No longer tangled up in the high drama of addiction, I settled into recovery. Clueless as to what normal people did to pass the time, I was depressed at my prospects. Sobriety seemed over-rated, linked with colors of gray, shut down to life's pleasures. In early recovery, I drifted toward the company of ex-addicts, falling back onto familiar patterns of gesture and speech, reminiscing about the past like a fabulous vacation in the South of France. Holding onto prehistoric feelings of inadequacy put me in a dangerous spot, and I struggled to move on, but where? At first, I felt condemned to a lifetime of boredom, some weird penitence for years of living on the edge. All my extra-curriculum activities centered around substance abuse, and now in recovery, I was at a total loss.

One day, sitting on a cold metal chair in a church basement during a meeting I wanted to skip, someone shared a newfound hobby with such passion, I sat up and took notice. Was it possible to get so excited about gardening or hiking or painting or skiing? It sounded hokey, but their tone was sincere and enthusiastic, with body language to match. It planted a seed of possibility.

It was suggested that we revisit old hobbies and interests, past activities that brought delight. Growing up on the beaches of Long Island, water sports played a role—floating on oversized inner tubes, swimming, and hanging at the beach with girlfriends, all healthy pleasures. At sleep-away camp, my skills got serious with canoeing, sailing, and waterskiing; the water held no fear. Cancer is my astrological sign, and I always felt a calmness at the water's edge. Sailing became a spark that grew into a passion.

When I was active, my best relationships were with drugs and the people I got them from. Newly sober, I was at a loss as to how to connect. I could only explore so far without taking the plunge—meeting new people. It felt scarier than scoring on Brooklyn's Metropolitan Avenue in broad daylight. Signing up for sailing classes, joining a club, going to boat shows, and—horror among horrors—asking to sail on someone's boat were all daunting prospects. For a person who was crazy-fearless without blinking an eye, says truckloads about the challenge to change feelings. The measurement of that dread was directly proportional to the lengths traveled to recover from old fears. My passion for sailing opened the door to the woman I was hoping to be—the true me.

*****

2000, *The Foxsea*

As financially secure as my next paycheck and monthly child support made me, I dreamed of owning a sailboat once more. On breezy, sunny days, I'd fantasize that my ex had passed away, and I'd cashed in the substantial life insurance. A pipe dream was more like it. I was commemorating a decade of divorce and single parenthood, and I deserved a significant reward. What are the anniversary gifts for five years, or ten years? Wood and aluminum? A boat had all those elements!

My life as a single, sober mom revolved around my daughters, AA meetings, and work. I was past due for some joy, ASAP. By joining the local yacht club, I hoped to forge new friendships and invitations to sail. Sadly, that summer, I was asked only once to join the crew, as the main activity at the club was drinking. Surrounded by ladies, always with a full wine glass in hand, and husbands constantly sipping beer, I felt like an outcast and did not connect.

The next spring, good fortune snuck up through a call from my great Aunt Edith, announcing a gift of $5,000 now instead of after her death, as inheritances from my maternal side had a way of disappearing. She had lost her only granddaughter, a cousin, to an overdose, and was sensitive to my situation, making us close. Tormented with newfound riches, ideas about how to spend it were tossed around the dinner table like a dinghy on rough seas. Curtains were much needed for the windows facing a busy street. The carpet needed replacing—or maybe we should take a vacation? But to me, it meant one thing, a sailboat. Living along the coastline, plenty of used boats were available in the area, and as luck had it, good friends were selling their Ensign, the same model my husband and I had owned when married.

"Forget about a boat, Mom, let's buy a new TV. This one's ten years old!"

"Mommy, you promised a set of monkey bars in the backyard!"

"Mom, Mom, did you see the new Delia's catalog? The skirts are awesome!"

"Mommy, we could buy a dog!"

A few mornings later, my oldest came down to breakfast, sloe-eyed and sleepy, recounting a dream from the night before. "I walked into the backyard, coming home from school, and sitting on the patio was a sailboat, perfect-looking except it was missing the sails."

Always hopeful for a premonition, she got my attention, and I inquired, "How big a boat, and was there a man at the helm?"

"Mom, it's only a dream." Her eyelids fluttered in disdain. "Anyway," she continued, "hanging on the windows in the living room were new white curtains made from the sails of the boat sitting in the backyard!"

Holy gift of the Magi, my dilemma had manifested itself in my daughter's dream! So, I did what every good sailor would do and spent more than I could afford, hook, line, and sinker, intuitively knowing that sailing would save me.

*****

The life of an addict resides at ground zero, void of a personal landscape. Cultivating hobbies and interests are important stepping stones to life-affirming behavior, opening the door to new friendships. Sailing has a clandestine language all its own, essential to learn with others ready to teach. The spirit of camaraderie surpassed my original expectations. Forging out onto the water, the crew relies on each other's skills, knowledge, and personalities to heighten the day. Water rushing, halyards flailing, and soaking spray transported me to new heights of sheer delight—while stone, cold sober.

A few summers ago, I crewed on a friend's boat for the Around Long Island Regatta, thrilled for the invite, a testimony to my skill and acceptance—like the Knights of the Round Table, noble and skilled! The day started early; we motored under five bridges, powering down the East River to the Statue of Liberty. The wind picked up at the mouth of New York Harbor, at the starting line with a hundred sailboats wildly jockeying for a good starting position—the tension in our hearts was palatable. Hitting the mark perfectly, we took off in a spirited downwind reach, and later, sprawled out in the cockpit, congratulated ourselves for taking the lead in our division.

Afternoon approached dusk, the breeze picked up, and I climbed forward on the deck to admire the South Shore beaches at an angle only seen from ocean racing. Suddenly, the noise of metal separating from fiberglass sounded, and I watched in awful, slow motion as the front stays flayed away from the bow of the boat. I remember trying to scream but was speechless with fear. After catching my breath, I shouted to lower the sails, or the mast would pull out. We took action, dropped the sails, and were now out of the race, as turning on the engine is a disqualifier.

Backtracking to the starting line under power on rolling waves was not pleasant, but soon things got worse, as Murphy's law took over when the engine failed and cut off the generator.

Quiet conversation punctuated the silence as we contemplated our situation of no running lights in the busiest shipping lane of supertankers this side of the Atlantic. Even with flashlights strapped onto the deck and navigating as best as we could, we were moving less than five knots an hour. I never felt further from home, finally understanding Dorothy in The Wizard of Oz clicking her heels and muttering "There's no place like home." Why didn't I have a will? I wondered at that moment. God, what will happen to the children? My mind plunged into chaos darker than any detox or withdrawal. My sailing mate never skipped a beat. My muteness gave him a chance to talk about work, divorce, and how his kids got along with his new girlfriend. Flashing on my beautiful garden and what to plant in the fall, my mind moved on—and off that horrendous anxiety—naturally and smoothly.

Ultimately gliding onto Ellis Island, we repaired the engine with enough power to motor up the East River toward Long Island Sound and our north shore harbor. Weathering this nautical event unearthed a resilience and faith never known to me. The repetitive day-in, day-out adherence to sobriety, at times a roller-coaster ride, blessed me with the sturdiness of mind to hang on, not panic, and just sit tight. The countless meetings I didn't want to go to, riding out the waves of old impulses, touched me with an honest spirituality, helping me to deal with adversity.

Enduring each adversity, a tiny gem on its own, strung together into a necklace of seamless sobriety, is priceless. Amazingly, the idea of picking up a pill or a drink never happened. Today, the voice of reason resides in my head, miraculously ousting the rationalizing lunatic that dominated that real estate for decades.

*****

Going out on the water, you're forced to leave all troubles onshore to better focus on sails, ropes, and tides. After each excursion, I returned more confident to handle life's curveballs and unexpected crises. Sailing offered fresh perspective with physical and emotional release, perfect for a recovering addict. Mundane fears of overdue bills or lack of romance took a back seat to the winds blowing out of the Northeast. I felt grateful to be back on dry land and welcomed the chaos and piles of dirty laundry waiting at home.

By sailing, I learned to measure my actions at the helm, riding out the waves of Long Island Sound and old junkie attitudes. The countless meetings I wanted to skip or dreaded phone calls made anyway gave me that confidence and the knowledge that I could do this. Testing my resolve with each sailing adventure instilled the sturdiness to hang on and not give up before the miracle happens.

Simple interests, close at hand, brought a steady hum of satisfaction, joy, and comfort. Cultivating interests that define me brought me back into the world. I love that part of me the best. Passion colors my life today. Adding weight to the balance of happiness and contentment tips the scales toward serenity and a quality of life not possible when you are strung out.

*****

Hungry Mother Tips

- Being sober is not enough to float your boat. Camaraderie and enthusiasm are needed to fuel your journey.
- Discover life-affirming activities. Get out there and look. You have to be in it to win it!
- Fortune favors the brave! Challenges yield newfound confidence to ride out adversity.
- Be bold and tickle your fancy with a hobby or interest that releases unabashed, unbridled joy!

Benefit Of Cooking

An appetizer that appears like an honored guest, wrapped in a golden puff pastry, makes a festive statement. This dish travels well; one big wheel of cheese on a flat tray, large enough to hold crackers, can feed any size crew.

Hungry Mother Recipe: Baked Brie with Candied Fruit

This recipe works best with the regular kind of brie you find at the supermarket. Choose any flavor of fruit preserve for the topping. Orange or ginger marmalade will give you something tangier than, say, raspberry or cherry jam, which are sweeter, more mellow

Ingredients

1 piece of brie, 8 to 12 oz., cold

1 sheet puff pastry, chilled but not frozen

3 tbsp thick jam/jelly/marmalade (any flavor) candied fruit: ginger pieces, orange peel, peaches or sliced pears

1 pear (cored and thinly sliced) or any fresh or dried fruit on hand

1 egg beaten with 1 tbsp water (egg wash for shiny finish)

1 tbs demerara sugar (optional)

crackers for serving (Carr's or any unsalted brand)

Directions

1. Heat the oven to 400 degrees. Using a large chef's knife, cut the white rind off the brie and discard (this works best when the cheese is very cold).
2. Roll the chilled dough to about 1/8-inch thick. Transfer the rolled dough to a baking sheet covered with parchment paper. Place the brie at the center

of the dough square and then spread the jam over the top of the cheese. Lay a thin layer of fruit on jam. Drape the four corners of the dough, one at a time, across the brie to enclose it. If there is too much overlapping dough, trim the sides before draping. You want the dough to just cover the brie.

3. Brush the egg wash over the brie, making sure it does not pool where it meets the tray, or it will stick. Sprinkle with the sugar if using. Bake on the middle rack of the oven for 35 to 45 minutes, until the pastry is golden brown and cooked through. Transfer to a wire rack and let cool for 8 to 10 minutes before serving warm.

Chapter 8

It's Okay to Fall

Recidivism

Good food is the foundation of genuine happiness.

~Auguste Éscoffier, French chef, revolutionized the culinary world

My name is Jane, and recovery karma has posted me as evening manager of this hormonal-bound halfway house in Boca Raton. In my thirty-five years of sobriety over forty years, it was the falling out and coming back that mark my spirituality. Recovery is ever-flowing, unpredictable currents colliding with time, compelling me to expel, retell, breathe in and out.

After my daughters grew up, I moved to South Florida with a passion to help recovering women transition from treatment to community living and then hopefully back home. Familiar with the rehab landscape of South Florida, and having recovery industry credentials, I secured employment as a halfway house manager. But there was another reason for moving—my sobriety was slipping. It was only a matter of time before I fell completely, devastatingly.

The empty nest syndrome of grown-up, independent daughters was kicking my butt. I knew it was my job to nurture and then give them wings, but why was it so painful? Combined with arthritic hips, soon to be replaced, I was on the edge of abusing prescribed pain meds.

Hearing one thousand stories of shattered relationships was a bottom I did not want to hit again. I needed an intervention ASAP, and I came up with this sober plan.

*****

2012, Boca Raton

At first glance, the women's sober house, a converted Florida motel, seemed at the intersection of out-of-luck and rock bottom. Arriving from rehabs near and far, the women landing here were teary-eyed or defiant, depending on their acceptance of the situation. From every age and economic reality, they'd wash up emotionally ship-wrecked on my watch as evening manager.

New residents congregated outside their apartments smoking, slumped over worn out, dirty broken chairs comparing stories. Language infused with strung-out street life, voices inflected with false toughness competed with cooing doves pecking at the scattered crumbs left by a thoughtful resident. Late at night, the women's cigarettes glowed on the balcony like flashing harbor buoys silently navigating the confluence of events that brought them here. Unfurling stories on the evening thermals of Palm Beach County, feelings were revealed in the first quiet time anyone could remember. Alcohol, drugs, the disease of more, makes mincemeat of natural instincts, smashing our internal compass, making us unable to find a way home.

Each of our stories begins with the substance of choice as an almighty liberator, the messiah delivering us from feelings of being alone and apart. The drug's warmth courses through on a cellular level, swaddling self-doubt and family history in a blanket of heavenly cotton, embracing broken souls with a love nothing else comes close to touching. Emotions governed by past events, planted by old voices that no longer matter, fester to a place of prominence. In our gut's darkness, disappointments go viral, filling voids like lichen on creviced rock. What starts out as soothing elixir cascades into the hunger—followed by relentless copping, scoring, hustling, lying, stealing, and prostituting for favors and money. Traveling any distance to get high, now it must be the opposite, going to any lengths to stay sober.

Late at night, a bed count was required, allowing a glance over their uneasy peace. In sleep's twilight, regret fluttered beneath eyelids as restless legs and toes touched rock bottom. Adored children and pets were left behind, never to be reclaimed. Ambition and home life cut short by drug addiction, friends and lovers lost to overdose. Young women released from prison for writing scripts, burglarizing neighbors, and vehicular homicide, now convicted felons. Some, with bodies scarred by near-death organ damage or crippling car accidents, use crutches and wheelchairs, never to recover. They ignored the red flags of manic behavior, changing relationships, jobs, hair color, geography, and sexual orientation, yet never considered quitting drugs. Ranting off to the few people who still cared, now alienated and alone—all had earned their bed here. I paused to let that image linger. It could have been me.

Recidivism, slipping and falling, go hand-in-hand with recovery, and statistically, there's a 50/50 chance it will happen to you. There's a difference between a slip and a fall. One is a brief spontaneous event, usually followed by regret. Relapse, on the other hand, happens when recovery is completely abandoned, and we go back to old habits. Suppose you're on a diet, and in a moment of weakness, maybe at a party, you eat a piece of cake. It's a spontaneous decision, confined to that one time, and you immediately get back on your diet. That is considered a slip. On the other hand, if you buy a candy bar, eat a pint of ice cream, and completely give up your diet, that's relapse. Some say if you relapse, you'll go right back to where you left off, but usually, it gets worse. When someone has been abstinent, then starts up again at the original dose, all too often, it results in accidental overdose and death.

The disease of addiction is clever and cunning; day in and day out, it waits for a crack in my resolve. It can speak to me when recovery is going well, and believe it's under control, then it fools me into a false sense of sobriety security. Our addictions are smart and strong, performing military push-ups in the hallway outside any 12-step meeting. My sober reality is, I cannot take just one pill or one drink; there's no such thing as a satisfied addict or drunk.

Recidivism has haunted me for decades, the proverbial monkey forever on my back. Why didn't they tell me that when I was first getting high? I can't predict when my disease will call out my name, and I will listen. One year or ten years sober, there is no telling when some hawker will call me back to the blackjack table and will place my money down, whispering for me to bet everything cherished—children, home, the trust of friends, and hobbies that mean so much to me.

One Saturday night, everyone checked in without incident except Sophie. She called at eleven with a lame excuse, signaling a long night for me. By now everyone was asleep except for the insomniacs smoking by the pool and the danger junkies waiting for stragglers. Secretly, they hoped shit would happen and they could witness it first-hand, as weekend curfews were a hotbed of drama.

The only staff on duty, I was shadowed by vague anxiety of all Hell breaking loose as well as the thrill that came with that possibility. Still a danger junkie, the outlaw in me never completely left. Calling the supervisor at midnight, I was reminded of protocol and could not leave until the MIA returned. Shit, that owner was so cheap, and the wages so low, overnight staff kept quitting! In South Florida, the recovery landscape was a gold rush; anyone with half a credential could jump in, and cash in on loose regulations monitored by a cracker barrel mentality. All contributing to the largest number of drug rehab beds in the U.S. Over the past few weeks, extra beds mysteriously appeared in the apartments, putting the halfway house over capacity. I was originally hired to manage twenty-five women; that night, it was thirty-five.

Miss MIA finally straggled in at one a.m., spewing run-on sentences about visiting her children living with a grandmother and losing track of time—not! Something was amiss—rumpled appearance, no eye contact, and a laissez-faire attitude. She was definitely high. *Selfish, stupid bitch!* Didn't she realize motherhood was a gift, an incentive to stay sober? After decades of tallying up those who achieved long-term sobriety and those who didn't, sober moms came out as the winners. Motherhood gives purpose to life, a reason to stay sober for the greater good. If only that woman could listen to the instinct of motherhood long enough not to give up and pick up. When a mommy fails at recovery and chooses drugs over children, they inherit a dysfunctional destiny.

If a resident is late, protocol mandates a drug screen and I get Sophie to peacefully pee in a cup. Of course, she denies getting high up to the end but when it reads positive for heroin, begins cursing and kicking the furniture. The consequences are immediate discharge either to a detox facility or the curb. I have to inform her family and call her dad whose response nearly matches hers. Unable to afford this stint, it's tough love now because he's done paying for unsuccessful results.

Meanwhile, all the commotion woke everyone up and out of bed, and residents were now hanging over the balcony and onto every word. Hormones in tandem with traces of mental illnesses and lingering withdrawal created a three-ring psychiatric circus, and I was the proud master of ceremonies, turning my craziness into a badge of courage and emotional strength. Five nights a week, my job was to mark that line in the sand, shake it down, and challenge those who crossed it. God damn it, I knew it would be two a.m. before I got out of there. Karmic payback was a bitch!

*****

Recovering people are starving for a life that matters, praying it's just not something to be endured. The odds of staying sober under those conditions are slim. While managing halfway houses in Boca Raton, I witnessed firsthand the importance of culinary activities for the recovering person. At the start of transitional living, there's an urgent need to change gears and replace a lifetime of bad habits and life-threatening pleasures. Residents learning basic life skills, perhaps for the first time, find themselves responsible for cooking, shopping, and maintaining a kitchen. What better vehicle than the culinary experience to learn a healthy balance?

Cultivating hobbies and interests are stepping stones to life-affirming behavior, essential for long-term recovery, and cooking becomes a chance to experience goals in an edible, tangible way. Money spent, time invested, and commitment compel the residents to complete the task, practicing competency in real-time. The basics of keeping the kitchen clean and a refrigerator full begin to strike a deeper chord.

Finding healthy pleasures in sobriety is serious business, as the consequences of insufficient amounts inevitably lead to recidivism. Healthy distractions from the mindset of slipping or relapsing are important to sustaining sobriety—move a muscle, change a feeling. Whether attacking a pile of dirty laundry, going for a walk, or baking a special treat, I know how to change the subject and move away from those destructive feelings. Culinary activities offer a chance to pause, change focus, contemplate, and most importantly, talk me down from that precarious ledge. Cooking is a delicious sobriety safety net to share with those I love.

*****

Hungry Mother Tips

- Recidivism is a monkey on my back. Addiction is ever-strong, doing push-ups in the hallway outside any 12-step meeting. Remain ever vigilant.
- Move a muscle, change a feeling. Attack a pile of dirty laundry or cook a sauce. Build up a treasure trove of

healthy distractions to change the mindset of picking up. It will pass.

- Motherhood is an incentive to stay sober; the odds are in your favor. Envision your children's lives without you and tap into that maternal spirit to get through rough moments.
- Cultivate interests and hobbies ASAP! The odds of sustaining sobriety are slim without them. Replacing a lifetime of bad habits does not happen overnight; make it a priority.

Benefit Of Cooking

This is one of my most challenging recipes and the most delicious, reserved for special occasions like New Year's Eve and my birthday.

Hungry Mother Recipe: Dot's Lemon Mousse

With only five simple ingredients, it's essential to follow the steps exactly to give it its fluffy, cloud-like texture and lemon sweetness. The difference between folding and mixing in this recipe is the difference between an elegant dessert and a creamy lemon glop. I've made this recipe many times over the years and still need to clear the decks emotionally to ensure success. It takes 60 to 90 minutes to assemble and should be refrigerated overnight, but in a pinch, a few hours will do. The results will be magnificent and memorable to all.

Ingredients

2 cup heavy cream for whipping
8 eggs*; separate yolks and whites
1/2 cup fresh lemon juice
1 1/3 cup sugar
1 envelope unflavored gelatin or tablespoon agar-agar (vegetarian)
Water

* Have extra eggs on hand in case you have to start again, as life happens!

Directions

1. Let eggs stand at room temperature for an hour; it's easier to separate yolks and whites. Have two bowls

ready for cracking eggs. Use the largest bowl for the yolks and the second largest bowl for whites. Do not contaminate egg whites with yolks; you may have to start over as the whites won't whip up properly.

2. Pour cream into a third bowl; make sure the bowl is big enough for whipping cream, which increases in volume. Put the mixer on high speed, turning the bowl frequently, incorporating any liquid on the bottom. Whip until soft peaks are formed; test periodically by turning off the mixer and checking the consistency.
   NOTE: Do not overmix as cream can turn into butter and become unusable. Cover bowl with plastic wrap, a lid or kitchen towel; place in refrigerator.
3. Beat egg whites at highest speed, capturing any liquid on the bottom of the bowl until stiff peaks are formed, resembling meringue.
   NOTE: Check periodically, as overmixing will turn it back to liquid and make it unusable for the recipe, but any overmixed whites can be used another time for scrambled eggs. Takes approximately 5 minutes. Cover and refrigerate.
4. Set up a small pot on the stove; fill ½ way with water. Place the Pyrex measuring cup in the pot; water should reach the middle of the cup, similar to water placement in a double boiler pot. Add ¼ cup water to the Pyrex cup, bring to boil, then slowly stir a small amount of gelatin or agar-agar. Stir well with a fork, making sure to dissolve before adding more. Let it cool briefly.
   NOTE: Must be a clear liquid; if not, use a small strainer to catch any lumps.
5. Beat egg yolks on low speed; gradually pour in

sugar a little at a time, making sure it is incorporated before adding more. Should resemble custard. Slowly add lemon juice with the mixer on low speed. Add gelatin (agar-agar) with the mixer on low speed. Mix thoroughly.

6. Take whipped cream from the refrigerator and *slowly fold into* egg yolk mixture.
   NOTE: Do not mix or stir; gently folding the whipped cream helps to retain its volume, which is key. Fold in with rubber spatula from top to bottom, making sure all ingredients are well blended.
7. Finally, fold in the whipped egg whites gently with a spatula to the egg yolk/whipped cream mixture.
   NOTE: Do not mix or stir; fold gently.

Special Equipment

Hand or standing mixer

Three large mixing bowls in different sizes; extra-large, large, medium

Pyrex measuring cup

Small, fine mesh strainer

Chapter 9

Working Moms
Make the Kitchen Work for You

We go through our careers and things happen to us.
Those experiences made me what I am.
~Thomas Keller, American chef, restaurateur, and cookbook writer

Advancing my career as a single, sober mom with young children was a pipe dream. I had to accept that reality while holding onto the hopeful expectation that as they grew up, new opportunities would arrive. It was hard on my ego, as in better times, I thrived in the workplace and wanted the boost that a good job and paycheck brought. When I was less than one year sober, I started working at an advertising agency again, my ego kicking good judgment out the window. Resurrecting that career was a poor choice for a mom managing school-age children. Adding a chaotic job when my reservoir of energy was already low from a busy life was a relapse waiting to happen. The need to overdo nearly put me over the edge and I had to recognize, I did not have to be a supermom. There were too many parts to my life, and being newly sober, I couldn't risk placing unrealistic demands on my limited energy.

*****

1998, Advertising Agency

Fevers, boo-boos, teacher conferences, carpooling to after-school activities, play dates, school vacations, and holidays all had priority over a career. If your job is time-sensitive or requires traveling or frequent trade show attendance, think twice about leaving at 5 p.m.

"Is there a problem at home?" was a question I heard often. "We have a deadline!"

Geez, no, I was just trying to have a family life. It seems my powers of concentration diminished exponentially after 4 p.m., the notorious witching hour for school-age kids.

Over the speaker, I often heard something to the effect of: "Jane, your daughter on line 1."

As soon as I lifted the phone off the cradle and pressed the blinking button, the questions/complaints would start:

"Mom, what time are you coming home? I hate this babysitter. Your other daughter stole my CDs again. There's no food in the refrigerator. Think I caught a cold. My blood sugar is 300. I need a booster of insulin. When are you coming home!?"

Again, the receptionist chimed in: "Jane, your other daughter on line 2."

Placing the first line on hold, I pushed the second button on the panel.

"Mom, two kids in my class are sick with chickenpox, and there's a rash on my stomach."

Ahhhhhhhhh!

This dialogue was reminiscent of Groucho Marx, The Three Stooges, and Abbott and Costello. Take your pick; it doesn't matter. It was a major f-ing calamity, and I had the lead role in this comedy of errors. What the Hell? I was desperate for good reviews as a sober mom while trying to earn a paycheck!

Times like those were as good a time as any for a low, sexy chuckle, daaarrling! Otherwise, I would have been crying hysterically. What was a mother to do? Commuting home in the car later that day, I started to laugh—a thunderous roll up from my belly and behind the stretch marks where it all started. Humor was strength. Didn't insanely happy sound better than just being insane? Did I have any unfilled prescriptions anywhere? Maybe I could stop off somewhere for a drink? Naaah, I needed a meeting!

*****

There are many parts to raising children, and it takes superhuman strength to keep that machinery running under normal circumstances. Being a responsible employee meant showing up with few excuses and maintaining the constant awareness needed to manage a family schedule. Contingency plans for sick days and holidays were a must! And our one-hundred-year-old Victorian house, like a horse, had to be fed every day. From checking the oil burner to repairing the washing machine, the house had its own to-do list.

Increasingly, daily 12-step meetings got pushed aside, and saving quiet time to read or reach out to peers was used for napping instead. Keeping recovery in my schedule while working was an overwhelming challenge. If we relapse, nothing else matters, and family life will slip away. I've heard too many stories of good intentions gone bad. I had to take my inventory and a hard look at my priorities. What was more important: career or sober motherhood?

Something had to change. The need to do it all, be a supermom, could put me over the edge again. I was there five years ago when I relapsed behind codeine. This was my second time around, and I finally realized being over-tired was my trigger point, a true threat. My addictive thinking rationalized a bizarre entitlement to pharmaceutical relief. Expending all this energy on children, the house, and work... Didn't I deserve a break? Knowing that instant relief was only a swallow away, a burst of happy energy to get through dinner and the girls' bedtime called out to me, louder each day.

At first, it felt unfair, double jeopardy. Motherhood and sobriety were interfering with the career goals I held onto. I searched for women's meetings and was not disappointed. It took many conversations with sober moms to acknowledge that a job didn't define me. Building a community of support with other moms was a chance to learn what worked for them. In that judgment-free zone, we shared feelings and situations, and their reality-tested feedback was the best advice I could hope for.

Because of my willingness and desperation, I was able to change old attitudes and find jobs that worked for me. I searched for businesses that appealed to another side of me: interests, hobbies, or a subject I wanted to learn more about. That opened jobs in horticulture, culinary, retail sales, and even sailing. There was something freeing about an hourly wage in the horticulture business—working around flowers and plants and being outdoors were stressbusters. Arriving home physically tired, I could rally after a hot shower and a few minutes of downtime. Being on my feet, working with things, not people, reduced work-related stress. At shift's end, I left it all behind with enough emotional energy for the second half of my day—supper, homework, and bedtime.

Silently joking about having so many different resumes, my work history seemed practically schizophrenic. I had the smarts and savvy for a corporate career, but for now, sobriety and parenthood came first. In time, I'd get a second chance, but there would be no second chances to raise my daughters. At times, embarrassed about wearing a logo-work shirt or apron, I worried about appearance. But the disgrace and shame of addiction were far greater. Duh, it was a no-brainer! I eased those feelings of low self-esteem by reminding myself of past achievements and learned to accept that my first job is sobriety, then motherhood, then career. It was not worth the risk.

*****

1980, Sotheby's Soufflé

Media planning at ad agencies is all about numbers, and since math was never my forte, I began to flounder. Getting fired was around the corner, and my street smarts said it was time to bust a move. Drug-free for three years and armed with the enthusiasm of the newly sober, I was ready for a better job. Gossip is an information tool, and like my old outlaw days, I put an ear to the ground and listened for the beat of hooves in the distance. My mother's nickname was Jungle Drums, and we teased that, when tilting her head out the window, my mom could hear the latest gossip blowing in the wind from Kings Point. My tribe took pride in storytelling, the gift of gab. Who needs a phone?

That policy is true in the workplace, too, and I gathered snippets in elevators, ladies' rooms, lobbies, and, of course, P.J. Clarke's across the street. Whispers overheard at the bar, laced with expensive Scotch, bragged about landing a fabulous new job from an executive search firm and I used that info to get interviews.

The eighties were all about "preppies," and I followed suit with a wardrobe from Brooks Brothers, complete with oxford shirts avec Peter Pan collars and tiny bow ties from the boys' department. I snagged an interview for an in-house agency seeking an advertising manager at Parke-Bernet's auction house on Madison Avenue, soon to be Sotheby's on York. *Whoa, there, cowgirl,* my mind cautioned, *can you make the leap from leafy cargo to illuminated manuscripts, marketing world-class art to a society consumed with lineage, patronage?* Hell, if I could cop dope in Hunts Point and run pot from Arizona to Points East, I could blend in and order lunch from 3 Guys on Madison—*their soups are legendary, daarrling*. The fates were kind as redemption rewards the reformed.

The advertising director was one of three Jews in this bastion of Mayflower lineage. Sensing we were from the same tribe—loyalty is always a valuable asset—she hired me as advertising manager. It was like a different world. Who were these blonde beings from Greenwich, and where the hell was Trinity College? Introduction to WASPs was not on my college curriculum, and I only knew Ivy Leaguers from

Vietnam War protests. These Sotheby's girls were in a holding pattern for marriages forged at birth by family, and they scoured *The New York Times* Sunday society section as if reading a list of the dead and wounded from the war front.

Assimilation into the likes of Muffy, Buffy, Morgan, and Lucy required serious observation, and utilizing past skills of spotting narcs and rip-off artists became a valuable asset. "Act as if," that venerable mantra from drug rehab, translated to "behave as if" in this new world, and I copied mannerisms, speech patterns, and dress code. Who says no good can come from bad?

Celebrating my first week on the job, this Jewish girl's fancy turned to food, and I treated myself to a Rueben sandwich for lunch at my desk. My grandfather, born on Delancey Street, taught me the difference between pastrami and corned beef during our monthly visits to Katz's Deli. Now, the room went strangely quiet, and overheard Muffy report to Dale, "I just had a toommaatoo with plain yogurt and melba toast and am too stuffed!" My jaw went slack mid-bite as I suddenly realized I was surrounded by candidates for the Olympic trials of x-ray physiques, Nancy Regan being their poster girl. Obviously, this had not been a class of sports practiced in my neck of the woods, where "Essen mein kinder, essen" was the official team cheer, followed by the older but ever-popular, "Izzie, Ikey, Jakey, Sam, we're the boys that eat no ham, yay, City College!" Thoughts of deli sandwiches flew from my head, and I silently groaned over a future of chopped salads, hold the dressing.

Timing is everything, and the art market's slow burn turned to a sizzle when Parke-Bernet Galleries, facing competition in the New World, opted to merge with Sotheby's. Switching to in-house advertising with new staff opened the mahogany door long enough for me to enter the rarefied world of legendary collections and new money.

At first, I felt like a sideshow freak, fresh from addiction to this new world. "Step right up, ladies and gentlemen. Meet the new manager of advertising, coordinator of regional office activity, your favorite rehabilitated space cowgirl, yowser, yowser, yowser!"

Martha (as in Stewart) caters hors d'oeuvres at pre-auction events. The elegant ladies who lunch exclaim " oh how clever to use scooped-out cabbages for a dip" as they clambered over each other for the stuffed endive on their way to set record prices for all categories of art. From American painters to American Indian art, each success translated to bigger advertising budgets, and I, amazingly, was in the catbird seat. Directors of glossy, oversized art magazines wooed our lunchtime dance cards with hopes of advertising revenue. Les Pleiades, Café Carlyle, Polo Lounge, Odeon, and Balthazar became familiar territory, similar to the high life of Tucson.

Jack and Meryl in from the coast, and Richard straight out of *American Gigolo,* along with a cast of hundreds, mixed with the very oldest and newest money to peek at pre-auction exhibitions. In 1982, the production team of *In the Still of the Night*, a film noir about a murder at an auction house, sent a location scout to my apartment for set design tips. Japanese *Vogue* photographed my accessories and had me stand on a Park Avenue island and throw a red straw hat in the air, very Mary Tyler Moore. Sotheby's senior VP took me to the opening of the new Sculpture Garden at MoMA. Committing my budget to run monthly ads in *Interview* resulted in invitations to Warhol events from the Factory on Union Square to the Limelight. My connections were dazzling but humbling, not too shabby after socializing with junkies four years earlier.

Warhol had been building his personal inventory of paintings, antiques, and collectibles quietly for years. In 1980, a photo editorial of his 66th Street townhouse cache threw fashionable society into a feeding frenzy. Canvases leaning causally in piles of twos and threes, stacked against the wall without being hung, screamed, "Too much is never enough!" Art consumption scaled new heights, fueled by a bull market headed by Japanese industrialists, Saudi princes, and Jay McInerney's young Turks. The passionate obsession for art and antiques headed into overdrive, and I was front row and center.

Subconsciously paranoid of my reformed identity, I ascribed to "the best defense is a good offense" policy and worked late, dressed great, and formed strategic alliances. Voraciously reading back issues of *Town & Country, Architectural Digest,* and the *Society Blue Book*, I learned to substitute my Great Neck "Jewish American Princess (Japanese)" accent for a waspy stiff upper lip (Locust Valley Lockjaw). By the time Sotheby's dubbed me assistant vice president, my transformation was complete. And in true Sotheby's fashion, three years later, I became betrothed, pregnant, and retired from full-time employment.

*****

Being qualified for a variety of jobs turned out to be a blessing in disguise. I was able to secure employment with flexible hours, and if necessary, leave early without getting fired. Single, sober parenthood was stressful enough; I'd have been crazy (addictive thinking) to add to that burden.

Playdates make a difference, and those connections led to friendships with moms in my neighborhood. Meeting the mothers of my daughter's friends expanded my social circle, a win-win situation. Reaching out to other moms did not come easy, but my desire to cultivate friendships for my daughters forced me out of my shell. Playdates are a vehicle for parents, too, giving everyone the chance to evaluate each other—to assess if your house is a firetrap, if there are empty liquor bottles strewn about, or if you answer the door in a thong. These casual appointments are a form of currency for working moms, and the accumulation of credit helps to avoid childcare disasters. Swiss banking is child's play compared to the etiquette required.

So get your act together for the sake of everyone's social life. Make that phone call you've been putting off. Your self-worth is not on the line; it's just an insert on the calendar. Otherwise, you'll be stuck with your kids more often than you can handle.

*****

Hungry Mother Tips

- Avoid the supermom syndrome. Recovery cannot be the last item on a to-do list.
- Cook smart. Plan ahead, and stock up on essential ingredients. Make the most of your freezer.
- Dinner on busy nights should tickle your fancy too. Pick something you like.
- Build up credit in the playdate bank. Invite their friends over whenever possible—extra points for serving dinner.

Benefit Of Cooking

Living in close proximity to New York City, I have the benefit of enjoying many ethnic cuisines, and this dish is my all-time favorite. Easy and quick to assemble with ingredients always in my pantry, it offers a pause of satisfaction after a hectic day. It's important for my well-being, too, that dinner brings a smile to my face and tummy.

Hungry Mother Recipe: Cold Sesame Noodles

Twice the fun when everyone uses chopsticks. Use any kind of crunchy vegetables on-hand to bring color and nutrition. Sesame noodles can be paired with any protein available; I, for one, keep my freezer filled with chicken sausage and turkey or salmon burgers, all easily defrosted and heated up.

Ingredients

2 cups chopped crunchy raw vegetables: snow peas, bell peppers, cucumbers, scallions

1 lb. (box) of long, pasta-like linguine

2-3 tbsp dark sesame oil

1/2 cup tahini, peanut butter, or a combination of the two

2 tbsp sugar

3 tbsp soy sauce or to taste

1 tbsp rice or white wine or other vinegar

2 tsp minced garlic (optional)

1-2 tsp minced fresh ginger (optional)

1 tbsp sesame seeds or chopped peanuts (optional)

Directions

1. Bring a large pot of water to a boil and salt it. Add noodles and cook until barely tender, about 5 minutes. They should retain a hint of chewiness. Drain,

rinse with cold water, drain again, and toss with a splash of sesame oil.

2. Prepare the vegetables: trim, seed, peel as necessary, and cut into bite-size pieces. Reserve in a container until ready to use.
3. In a medium bowl, whisk together the remaining 2 tbsp sesame oil, the soy sauce, rice vinegar, sesame paste, peanut butter, sugar, ginger, and garlic.
4. When you're ready to eat, toss the noodles and the cut vegetables. Pour the sauce over the noodles and stir to coat.
5. Serve at room temperature. Sprinkle with sesame seeds or chopped peanuts.

NOTE: Extra sesame dressing can be stored in the fridge up to two weeks. Just mix well.

Chapter 10

Taking Inventory
Loving Yourself

Dining with one's friends and beloved family is certainly one of life's primal and most innocent delights, one that is both soul-satisfying and eternal.
~Julia Child, cooking teacher, author, and television personality

As a young woman, I believed love was the answer to life's problems. My self-esteem rose or fell depending on achieving it. Second-guessing my value based on having a boyfriend or not turned out to be a flawed theory. And those who found love seemed to carry a smug attitude as if, through sheer will and effort, they were saved from some unhappy destiny. Failing at love went beyond disappointment, moving to a deeper, more damaging territory, undermining my self-worth. Plagued by the angst of love enabled my self-doubt to run riot, giving way to feelings of unworthiness. At times, feelings of despair left me bereft and mourning the love I needed to be complete.

Looking back, I was uber-sensitive, hurt by the slightest rejection. The pursuit of love was an alienating process, and after an excess of experiences, I remained clueless. And most defeatedly, when someone loved me, I felt indebted for their kindness. A dangerous spot for a recovered woman. We're all a product of our upbringing, and my folks were well-meaning but narcissistic. Attending to them was my role, and parental praise came from anticipating their needs before they asked. Wanting to please, love evolved into an indentured servitude of sorts, conditional on being good, not about my essence. Hey! It was the '50s and '60s, not much enlightenment going on—there's no blame, only the time and place of my childhood.

Could or would anyone really love me? By my late twenties, recovered and integrated into society, I carried a warped view of relationships, something to avoid. An old voice from the Isle of Id chanted, "Only another ex-addict could love me." Any well-adjusted mate would surely discover a variety of flaws. Subconsciously, I pinned a scarlet letter to my chest, forever marked by a shameful past. It was going to be slim pickings to find a suitable husband. Approaching thirty, chords of desperation crept into my consciousness. It was not about being lonely or unhappy but a gnawing torment, of missing the great secret of life. The pursuit of love was elusive, and as it represented salvation, it possessed a frantic quality. Despite overcoming addiction, I felt a loser, hastily grasping at theories, remedies, and therapy, throwing me into a slow panic.

*****

1979, Bright Lights, Big City

Three years clean and sober, my resolve wavered. Living in a sweet walk-up apartment above Rosa Mexicana on East 58th Street, a good job at an advertising agency only blocks away, perched me on the pink cloud of sobriety. Leaving rehab, I was warned a hundred times that part of recovery is being prepared for the unexpected slip or setback, never knowing in what form or shape it will appear. One thousand, twenty-four hours later, reality arrived.

The advertising industry in New York City resembled Tucson—the money, the men, and the ambitious young Turks mimicked the Ol' Pueblo's weed dealers. It was the salad days of agencies, with oversized expense accounts and little oversight. As a media planner, magazines, TV, and radio stations pursued our advertising dollars. Every week, invitations for lavish events circulated the office, from cocktails on the *Forbes* yacht to Broadway show tickets, and of course, the three-martini lunch. The culture of TV's *Mad Men* was all true; serious drinking was accepted, nay, encouraged, to finalize a deal.

After-work drinks along Third Avenue were de rigor as *Saturday Night Fever* had exploded onto the big screen and into disco happy hours. Jay McInerney would chronicle that debauchery in *Bright Lights, Big City*; it was all true. I could not afford to get caught up in this real estate and fashioned a secret hustle of bonding with work buddies while passing up the comradery of "alcohol, toots, and tokes." Never revealing my true colors or announcing that "I don't drink," only nonchalantly turned down offers. Being a junkie wasn't so different, hiding true colors to get over on people; the feelings were remarkably similar.

Care to date alcohol-free?

Up until then, I'd never been intimate without drugs, adding another layer of anxiety to my normal jitters. Finding romance and a husband haunted my sober reality, and who went to Studio 54 sober? As a hippie chick, I enjoyed a colorful history of sexual experiences, but never once not high. Intuitively knowing only cats had nine lives, this pussy had exceeded her limit. Oy, vey, this Jewish girl's hamper was overflowing with dirty laundry, and self-doubt was a constant companion as I strove to live clean. My ego had suffered greatly over the years from humiliating psychiatric hospitalizations to whispered speculation among family and friends. Best to protect me from myself. I limited love affairs to guys in recovery or waspy men, who were not likely drug-takers and were intrigued by my sobriety, a challenge of sorts. "Meet Jane. She doesn't drink. Isn't that amazing? Do you play squash?" I felt the freak, the odd duck, a fish out of water as 12-step meetings were decades away from being in the hipster vernacular. I was a walking contradiction, an oxymoron.

Sober for three years, I arrived at the intersection of compromise and conviction. Increasingly, my days ended white-knuckled and spent. Navigating both worlds was exhausting. I was drifting to the dark side and saw red flags flapping in the wind. Disturbing landscapes appeared in my dreams, and I awoke disoriented and sweaty. Walking in mid-town, unsuspecting side streets turned menacing with the scent of reefer, triggering olfactory memories that turned weed into Mexican Mud cooking up in a spoon. My anxiety on a cellular level was equal to the same strung-out feeling that overwhelmed me when I was overdue for a hit. It did not bode well. Finding sober love seemed impossible, and I soon felt betrayed by sobriety.

Enter a warrior who shared the same battle experience, the rehab director where I got sober. Freshly divorced, recovered, a Jewish Prince from Bronx's Mosholu Parkway, street-savvy and self-made from the same cloth as Calvin Klein, Ralph Lauren, and Gary Reiner, the attraction was real. Brilliant, charming, and witty, but most important, no holier than thou attitude without judgment. The stage was set to marry my program, believing an in-house counselor could save me. For a brief time, I felt secure and smitten with my life....

Hahahaha!

*****

As a divorced mom with young children, carving out a sober love life was a challenge, forcing me to grow in ways I never imagined. All this doubt caused me to examine my expectations and radically changed my definition of love. Deep down, the dating drama kicked up self-doubt in too many ways that could sway my sobriety. I had to let that go. Romantic relationships ebbed and flowed; if meant to stick, they would. What did I anticipate receiving from a loving relationship? And would I have the time? As a single, sober mom earning a paycheck, I barely had thirty seconds to brush my hair and put on lip gloss.

But there was good news. Being in recovery taught me how to reach out and move into the world. It compelled me to be open to fresh emotional concepts. Early on, we learn how to give of ourselves and, just as important, to receive—for me, though, that was easier said than done. In my old way of thinking, love signaled a one-sided relationship. In hindsight, I should have trusted my gut instinct. Instead, the growing anxiety of being thirty, unmarried, and no closer to being a mom tipped the scales toward an unwise decision. Sober thinking hadn't healed all my emotional scars yet, and the stigma of an unsavory past haunted my options. The familiar rhythm of pleasing and not getting much back was a comfortable, familiar place. So, naturally, I married a world-class narcissist so extreme that it only took a few short years for me to realize the mistake. I was lucky to be in recovery; otherwise, I'd still be afflicted with a restless discontent, chasing that elusive love high.

The gift of sobriety includes an ability to listen to inner dialogue, genuine realism, and our own truths. All that emotional and spiritual suffering gifts us with growth and the maternal maturity to shape our world. We've uncovered our bare roots, endured the pain and anxiety of sustaining sobriety, and now, with an eye to the future, can move forward in a different direction. I gained a new awareness of what love meant, all the while enjoying true love from my daughters, a family of friends, and the occasional romance. For me, personal relationships with friends and peers began to occupy a place of central importance versus any romantic ones. As I matured, dreaming of finding the one person who would complete me, no longer matched who I was, and I put my faith in other endeavors.

Love is the long game, a process, not a marathon or sprint. Oftentimes, while raising my daughters, I'd feel physically bankrupt but managed to dig deep into a reservoir of maternal energy. That was unconditional love. As a sober mom, being emotionally available when they were at their most vulnerable and reaching out became as involuntary as breathing. This gave rise to making all types of enduring connections with friends and acquaintances. Over the years, I've taken delight in watching my daughters affirm their values, blossoming into who they are today, lovely young women with a solid moral compass. Moments of sweet affection and reflection give me a fuzzy warm glow, only to make me realize I'm grinning ear to ear. All this feels like love. And as I age and get closer to the end we all face, I enjoy warm confidence that the love I've given will always come back. As the Beatles sang, "And in the end, the love you take is equal to the love you make," or vice versa. I do not worry about being lonely or unloved in the future.

Love is a motivating force and, combined with long-term sobriety, enabled me to redirect my life with purpose. Doing well by doing good goes to reinforce my sense of purpose and be in the world in a loving, giving way. The power of self-love morphed into willpower to self-direct toward a tangible goal. A new concept, something I adore about myself. That's self-love in a healthy, life-affirming way.

> *I go...to forge the smithy of my soul the uncreated conscience...*
>
> *~James Joyce*

Geez, it only took fifty years; at least I figured it out!

Every decade brings a new definition of love and relationships. Today's world is one of transition; all the familiar moorings are gone. With the rising problems of the present, there's an urgent demand upon the individual for personal responsibility. The Hungry Mother has a true advantage: courage and the capacity for withstanding uncertainty. We've discovered on a deeper level what it means to be human, substance-free, and ready to face our collective destiny. This state of flux and turmoil begs for a home-cooked meal, the common denominator of caring, connection, and encouragement.

*****

Hungry Mother Tips

- Never leave the house without looking in a full-length mirror.
- Utilize your in-house fashion patrol. Children are known for their honesty and undoubtedly possess a hipper fashion sense than you.
- Hope springs eternal, but sometimes, no relationship is better than a lousy one. Think of the extra closet space!
- Keep an emergency make-up kit in the car.

Benefit Of Cooking

Keeping one eye peeled for a romantic relationship can be a part-time, if not a full-time job. With heart and soul occupied with keeping the home fires burning, it's a Herculean task. Energy levels are dangerously low, and diverting reserves for romance is risky business. Following a night of lovelorn frustration, it's comforting to have the ingredients to assemble this dish.

Hungry Mother Recipe
Poached Pears:
Swanky Dessert or Sweet Salad

My weakness for sweets happens at night. I joke that my flannel nightgown becomes a magnet to the refrigerator, unable to resist its pull. After the girls are asleep and the house is quiet, I hunger for something cuddly, warm, and just for me. Pears poached in cream, butter, and sugar are the perfect foil. Watching through the window of the toaster oven, I'm mesmerized by sugar caramelizing into cream, a dreamy sensation to lure me to sleep. Using an individual baking dish (oval ramekin) reinforces my entitlement to a special dessert just for me and never fails to please.

Sweet Dessert

Ingredients

1 pear barely ripe but not too hard; Comice, Bartlett, or Bosc

1/4 cup heavy cream

3 tbsp sugar

2 tbsp butter

Nutmeg (optional)

Directions

1. Wash pear, cut in half lengthwise, and remove core/ seeds.
2. Bake in toaster oven, 350 degrees.

3. Put butter and sugar on the bottom of an individual baking dish (ramekin).

- Place pear cut side up on top and bake for 10 minutes until bubbling.
- Add cream to cover pear halfway, then bake another 5-7 minutes until gets bubbly again.
- Let cool before eating.

Swanky Salad

When the girls were young, I managed the nearby Bookmark Café (Oyster Bay), which boasted an elegant menu and wildly successful bookstore. It was a dream job, arranging book-signing events for authors, cookbooks being my favorite. From Ina Garten to Anthony Bourdain, the kitchen created special menus to match the visiting author's latest book. This poached pear salad of pecans and cranberries with a creamy blue/Roquefort or goat cheese dressing served on delicate greens makes me feel like a celebrity every time. A perfect mood changer when feeling blue and low.... Keep on hand to lift lovelorn spirits.

There are many recipes for a 'poaching liquid', feel the freedom to experiment and use whatever spices you have on hand, from cloves to star anise. Here's a simple approach:

Ingredients

1/2 cup sugar

1 large cinnamon stick

6 whole cloves

1 vanilla bean

Zest of an orange or lemon

Directions

1. Add enough water to cover pears halfway up.
2. Peel the pears, leaving the stems intact, and scoop out the seeds from the bottom with a sharp spoon or melon baller, taking care not to break.
3. Lay the pears on their sides in the poaching liquid and simmer for 20 minutes, carefully turning so all sides are cooked.
4. Remove with a slotted spoon. Let cool.

Dressing

I always use glass jelly jars for salad dressings, perfect for mixing and traveling with dressing on the side. Put all the ingredients except the cheese in the jar, close the lid, and shake vigorously. Whatever cheese you use, let sit at room temperature until soft, then mash in the jar with other ingredients; results are creamier, and the cheese is evenly distributed.

Ingredients

3 oz. blue cheese (Stilton, Roquefort) or goat cheese

2-3 tbsp white wine or apple or champagne vinegar (contains no alcohol). Do not use red vinegar.

1 tsp Dijon mustard (or any spicy mustard on hand)

1/4 cup good olive oil

2-3 tsp sugar or 1 packet sweetener

Salt & pepper to taste

Directions

Pour over salad and toss well.

Salad

Ingredients

1/4 cup cranberries

1/4 cup chopped nuts (walnuts, pecans, pistachio, or hazelnut)

Lettuce: delicate greens (arugula, frisee, endive, radicchio, bibb)

Directions

Put lettuce in an oversized bowl, pour dressing, and mix well. Place poached pears on lettuce, sprinkle with cranberries & nuts.

Chapter 11

Spirituality

Your Higher Power Is at The Table

I place food at the center of our humanity, as it nourishes not only our physical bodies but also our emotional and spiritual lives. Food is truly a cultural phenomenon that informs our traditions and our relationship with the earth. I genuinely believe that food connects us all.

~Éric Ripert, French chef, author, and television personality

The best part of getting sober is the relief from believing in a higher power and the possibility of hope. Hope is an essential commodity in recovery; without it, why bother? For me, it started as a glimmer of the possibility of becoming the woman and mother I always hoped to be. At first, my home group was my higher power; I attended with the sole purpose of staying sober and not failing. My commitment to converting old addict attitudes into life-affirming ones fueled the magic that happened in meetings.

Listening to my peers' struggles and successes—from exercising restraint to making amends to their families—all contributed to the hope of redemption. The promise of spiritual redemption remains a powerful motivator for me and is why I'm passionate about giving back to the recovery community. It's a vehicle to empower my purpose and, ultimately, to help me forgive myself.

Restraint and resilience are key to coping with adversity. Life is not static; its fluid and nothing stays the same—the weather, health, romance, finances; practically everything is subject to change. Resiliency prepares us for the next inevitable stressful situation.

Recovery navigates the river of circumstance and challenge; we must learn to adapt—to change or sink. Flexibility, going with the flow, and trusting that things will work out is a spiritual act of faith. "Let it go, let it go..." ("Let it go" from Disney's *Frozen*). "Let go and let God" (a common AA slogan). "'You can't always get what you want but if you try sometimes, you'll find, you get what you need" ("You can't always get what you want" by The Rolling Stones).

Nothing replaces the value of attending 12-step meetings.

The physical, tangible experience of listening to how recovery works for others while sitting with them side by side plants the seeds of spirituality. And changing our behavior for an abstract idea is also a powerful leap of faith. The person-to-person action of holding hands and praying together was a game-changer for me, resonating with a core belief I had lost touch with. Most 12-step meetings are held in places of worship and whisper something sacred, spiritual, and hopeful.

Newly sober, I felt an empty space, a vague spiritual craving that drugs had satisfied, and was missing a sense of belongingness and self-esteem.

The void where addiction once resided, that empty space, is where our spirituality can enter. When abstinence begins, that empty space, once occupied by addiction can transition into a space which can open into God. Those in sustained sobriety learn to rely on spiritual instincts to diminish anxiety and personal conflict while maintaining faith in the future. Making peace with our spiritual nature establishes meaning and purpose in our lives, essential in preventing recidivism.

> *The start of spirituality is changing our behavior for an idea, not a thing. Human beings are the only species to have the capacity to learn from history and contemplate the purpose of existence and ways to better ourselves. It's all about concepts, not things, that is existential*

thinking. Delaying gratification while considering the consequences of our actions, we have the capacity to make moral decisions. Which may result in denying ourselves behaviors that our bodies lust for. That is spirituality. When we exercise these uniquely human capacities, we are being spiritual and can be, without religion.

~Rabbi Abraham Twerski, addiction psychiatrist, author, and spiritual leader

What is the purpose of existence? What is my purpose? What is the point?

Each year, as I gained emotional distance from substance abuse, my spirituality grew, and with it, questions. Ask any recovering addict what it takes to stay clean. We'll rate spirituality over medical, rehab, or social services every time. We don't crave therapy; we want redemption!

What does existential thinking mean in sobriety? Addictive thinking is non-spiritual, the polar opposite of spirituality, and why recovery requires a shift from stinkin' thinking. We are each responsible for creating purpose and meaning in our own lives. Existentialism emphasizes action, offering the radical concept of free will, and makes decisions fundamental to human existence—a positive and reasonable purpose to hold onto and give meaning in our lives.

By nature, we are God-wrestling people, no matter what religion, and grappling with our existential needs puts us at a crossroads with our consciousness. We can choose our own purpose and shape our essence, as existence precedes essence. Products of past choices can be changed by choosing differently in the present, a spiritual leap of faith. Nothing fixes our purpose but ourselves, by choosing what is important to us. Being authentic is something we arrive at on our own; it is not given to us by gods, governments, teachers, or other authorities. Authenticity is significant to my spirituality, the truest expression of my inner spirit. Free will at last.

> *It is only after safety, belongingness, and self-esteem are achieved that self-actualization, the highest of these needs can be addressed. It makes sense that this spiritual awareness only happens after sobriety is sustained. The self lies midway between the unconscious and the conscious and we need to make peace with that spiritual nature, establish meaning and find comfort in life. The collective unconscious matures into constructive spiritual orientation and psychotherapy can help people achieve this enlightenment.*
>
> *~Abraham Maslow, American psychologist,*
> *Maslow's Hierarchy of Needs*

The gift of desperation.

As a mother, I was desperate to get this program right, understanding the lives at stake if I failed. At times after a meeting, I experienced physical heartache, leaving me with a gut feeling that if I deviated from this program, I would die. Without the gift of desperation, I would have continued to search for hope in all the wrong places. Those who study the Bible, Torah, or Koran intellectually believe that it is a suggestion to live a spiritual life. They do not experience that same gut feeling, that life itself is dependent on total adherence. For us in recovery, any deviation can result in institutionalization, jail, or death.

The physicality of meetings, the pleas, prayer, and worship in silent communion with my peers, feels real. The religious dynamic of AA demonstrates a sincere, selfless, fellow-feeling, inspired by peers who willingly awaken at night to help one another. That sense of responsibility is far superior to non-alcoholics in relation to families and friends, rarely found in traditional religious groups. My prayers sprung from the heart, a pure plea to get it right, for me and my daughters. A solid dose of desperation is a rare gift and makes Step 1 much easier to accept.

> *Once we are sober, we need something to give meaning to our lives, a sense of purpose, a purposeful life. The newly sober wrestle with spirituality and the 12-step community wrestles together but does not come to the same conclusion. It's a highly personal issue with each person an expert on its definition. A person has to make peace with his/her spiritual nature to establish meaning and find comfort in life.*
>
> *People in treatment, rate Alcoholics Anonymous more influential than medical care and counseling, believing the role of spirituality is critical to sustaining sobriety. Most of us believe that prayers can have a positive effect on our recovery and mental health professionals will agree that some larger force is at hand that makes sense of the mystery of the universe. In treating psychiatric disorders, belief in treatment is almost as important as the medications prescribed.*
>
> *~Dr. Marc Galanter, Professor of Psychiatry/ Addiction Studies Langone NYU School of Medicine, and author*

Why is it hard to be good?

All humans are imperfect by divine design. We are endowed with free will and challenged to choose between opposing inclinations, good and bad. Both come from God and are necessary to human existence. In the Jewish tradition, repentance is called *teshuvah*, translated as "returning from going astray." Repentance is a return to the path of righteousness comprised of three elements: confession, regret, and a vow not to repeat the misdeed. Each day, we struggle to take the right action and make amends. When we don't, it all goes to building spiritual muscle. Practicing the principles of the 12-steps is the same as, "Know God in all your ways, nothing is outside our relationship with God."

It's unfortunate that only addicts can avail themselves of the 12-step program.

~Rabbi Abraham Twerski

Belief in a higher power gifts/grants a way to repair our souls. In essence, those who return to God in repentance stand with the saintliest. Overcoming addiction gives us the freedom to recognize our imperfections, misdeeds, and vulnerabilities; we've learned to own and befriend them. By hitting bottom, we gain humility, integrity, and wholeness, finally seeing that sobriety is a life-affirming experience, not one of embarrassment and shame but a blessing in disguise.

*****

2011, Jewish Recovery Center

Living in Boca Raton, I discovered the Jewish Recovery Center and volunteered to help with their events. Every Friday night, we hosted a Sabbath dinner for the many Jewish residents from local rehabs, sober houses and their alumni who came for a Kosher feast. Led by Rabbi Meir, a charismatic fellow from the Brooklyn Chabad, it offered a chance to connect with Jewish people in all stages of recovery. Florida, with the most treatment beds in the country, saw an influx of Jewish people in recovery, from Canada to Chicago. Their families hoped to keep them connected to their faith by supporting the JRC, where holidays are celebrated in a Kosher environment while away in treatment. Additionally, many who recovered there have established sober roots and choose to remain rather than return home to the scene of the crime. As a result, the JRC remains a vibrant resource for the recovering Jewish community.

Most Friday evenings before sunset, I scooted to the synagogue with unexpected energy, setting up tables, putting out food, greeting guests, and then cleaning up. I always get pleasure from feeding a lot of people in a group setting. Despite the frenzied activity, I felt centered, serene, and had a sense of community, taking me by surprise as I did not consider myself religious.

The JRC established an annual retreat with world-renowned speakers and workshops. It was there, in 2011, that I met Rabbi Abraham Twerski, famous addiction psychiatrist, prolific author, and storyteller extraordinaire. We stood together in line for a dinner buffet. A tiny man dressed in elegant Hassidic garb—long silk coat, oversized fur hat—exchanged pleasantries with me in an expressive voice. I'd never met anyone like him.

Later that evening, he told a story about addiction and redemption, relating to the Torah, that left me awestruck. He explained how the transitional space, once occupied by addiction, now vacant, can be a space for spirituality, and eventually God, the beginning of an existentially meaningful life. Could it be as simple as declaring a belief in God, a vibrant optimism? It was a pivotal spiritual moment that, for me, had taken thirty years to evolve. That vague higher power of my 12-step program morphed into religious orientation. It connected the dots of my beliefs, maturing from protecting sobriety to guiding my spiritual life and ultimately to self-actualization, the last piece of the spiritual puzzle.

A few years later, after I moved back to Long Island during the height of the opioid epidemic, I connected with Rabbi Irwin Huberman. He was so concerned with the growing substance abuse surrounding his congregation that he flew to Florida to attend Jewish Recovery Center's annual workshop. Call it kismet, fate, or *beshert;* when an unexpected and nearly impossible event takes place, it is usually due to luck or divine intervention. As fate would have it, his temple was located in the same town I moved back to, and together, we created a non-profit sobriety resource for the Long Island Jewish community, nerali.org.

Shining the light of spirituality on the tragic, gritty reality of substance abuse within the safe sanctuary of a congregation goes to "break the stigma and start a conversation," the first step toward recovery. Providing support groups for family members with a loved one struggling with alcoholism and addiction is vital for coping with the stress of championing someone's recovery journey.

Addressing societal issues without prejudice and promoting social action go to expedite change. Encouraging dialogue contributes to a better understanding of alcoholism and addiction, contributing to the solution. Every community has a profound capacity to help when there is access to support groups and treatment resources.

> *It is time to bring recovery up from the basement into the Kiddush room.*
>
> *~Rabbi Huberman, Congregation Tifereth Israel, Glen Cove, New York*

*****

Hungry Mother Tips

- Addiction is the antithesis of spirituality.
- Desperation is a gift; let it work for you.
- Freedom of choice, free will, is only possible sober.
- Living a spiritual life leads to redemption and self-realization.

Benefit Of Cooking

Early on, raising my girls as a single mom, neighbors and friends gathered us under their wings with invitations to dinners, barbeques, and holidays. My dearest neighbors were Israeli, and there was always a seat at their table for us. And during the warm weather months, the smell of garlic on pita warming on the grill, signaling exotic hummus to follow, wafted into our backyard. In the late '80s, hummus was mostly homemade or from some mysterious store in Brooklyn. It was not readily available in stores as it is now, and I discovered this simple recipe.

Hungry Mother Recipe: Heavenly Hummus

The secret to a silky-smooth consistency is to taste it often. You'll learn to add a bit of oil, a drop of lemon juice, or a sprinkle of cumin, and at times cold water, to arrive at the consistency you prefer. This dip is a real crowd-pleaser served with pita bread, fresh vegetables, or chips, and always make extra portions to keep aside for yourself.

Ingredients

2 cups canned chickpeas well-rinsed
1/2 cup tahini, with some of its oil
2-3 tbsp extra virgin olive oil or substitute sesame, avocado, or any nut oil
2-3 cloves peeled garlic, or to taste
Juice of 1-2 lemons, plus more as needed
Salt to taste
1 tbsp ground cumin or smoked paprika
Dash of tabasco (optional)

Directions

1. Put the tahini, cumin or paprika, oil, garlic, and lemon juice in a food processor until blended to a consistent texture.
2. Add 1/3 of the chickpeas, pulse/blend into mixture, continue to add a batch of chickpeas until smooth.
3. Taste and add cold water, lemon juice, or even until a smooth puree. Feel free to adjust with salt, pepper.
4. Serve in a large bowl with crackers, chips, or crisp veggies.

Chapter 12

Service

Pay It Forward

Tell me what you eat, and I will tell you who you are.
~Jean Anthelme Brillat-Savarin, *The Physiology of Taste,* 1825

While managing sober houses in South Florida, I witnessed the positive impact of culinary activities on recovering people. Residents were responsible for maintaining a kitchen and the daily routine of preparing meals, many for the first time. Within the safety of a structured environment, cooking for oneself became an opportunity to learn the basic elements of food preparation. I took note of the attitudes and behavior that contributed to a resident's success in sustaining sobriety, and those who embraced culinary activities seemed better equipped to maintain a sober lifestyle.

Prior to admission, the active addict's only concern is getting high, with all efforts and resources focused on that end. Forgoing food for drugs is commonplace, as the financial factor of addiction takes an overwhelming priority over other expenses. In early abstinence, learning to set money aside for the necessities of rent, transportation, and food is a challenge. Once a week, we drove residents to the supermarket and supervised their purchases within a set budget, compelling them to be mindful about their food, a good start for awareness in all areas. Hunger is a powerful motivator to get your life on track.

There are tremendous benefits to a transitional arrangement after in-patient treatment, providing a middle ground between rehab and returning home. Living in a supportive environment with peers who are going through similar circumstances makes the transition less overwhelming, reducing stress and chances for relapse. Adherence to house rules provides structure and known expectations. A sober house is a place to practice healthy habits learned in treatment, free from the temptation of alcohol and drugs. Most importantly, it instills a sense of community and strong personal connections, both key to sustaining sobriety. Understanding the importance of maintaining contact with a sober community predicts better outcomes in recovery.

Every Sunday, family-style community dinners were held, offering a new way to connect with peers. Each week, residents were assigned to a different team and rotated the responsibilities of menu planning, shopping, prepping, serving, and cleanup. They get to experience in real-time what it takes to feed thirty, fifty, or seventy-five people. Long picnic tables were set up outside, conducive to conversation, though a challenge for some who were outside their comfort zone. But a free meal is hard to refuse, and soon, they began to take pride in their culinary abilities. These lessons in "entertaining," reinforced by good food and camaraderie, began to strike a deeper chord. It demonstrated in real-time the joy of eating the "fruits of your labor" and offered a glimpse into a sober lifestyle, a recovered life.

For over twenty years, CASA Columbia (The Importance of Family Dinners VIII, 2011) has documented how the positive impact of families eating meals together can deter substance abuse. The simple act of sitting down to a family dinner fosters high-quality relationships and better communication, lowering risks for smoking, drinking, or using other drugs. Residents in early recovery have little sober experience with the natural rhythms of friendships or family life. Participating in community dinners is an invitation to be a part of a larger group, reinforced by a good meal and easily duplicated in the real world. Making a meal for others signals a generous spirit and a commitment to generating satisfying relationships, an excellent example of what it takes to bond. Learning to incorporate alcohol-free food events into a routine is a readily accessible way to expand and brighten the socialization process of recovery.

Newly sober, we benefit from structure, especially if we design it. Rituals become an activity that evolves from a routine we've assigned importance to, serving us in significant ways. The daily routine of meal preparation offers a natural way to center our mind, build focus, and stay in the present, a valuable self-calming technique. Becoming physically engaged at that "trigger" moment of contemplating relapse is a valuable tool for reducing stress.

Healthy distractions are part of my sobriety "toolbox," skills to combat negative thoughts and produce a steady hum of contentment. For me, when anxieties rise, my spirit is soothed by baking, cooking, or just reading over the many recipes I've gathered, and whatever is made will not go to waste. Collecting jars and glass containers is a hobby, and happily packing up and dropping off extra portions to friends is a part of me that I adore! Rituals reinforce that sacred time and space, of understanding what is significant in life, the cornerstone of spiritual practices, necessary to support sobriety and enhance spirituality.

Science tells us a solution may lie in what we do for others, not ourselves. Kindness toward others goes a long way. Residents are encouraged to provide mutual support and encouragement to fellow peers in the house. Those who have been there the longest, and have more time in recovery, are expected to support new residents. This type of "giving back" is a new experience, leading the way into bonding, and the dynamics of helping others, make us feel good. When residents are ready to secure employment, volunteering at nearby food banks and non-profit gift shops is a recommended first step.

Something as simple as donating time to a cause other than our own can ease feelings of loneliness, broaden our social network, and be a bridge to the community. Recovering people seek new ways to represent themselves in a more flattering light—as engaged, present, and sober. Food is a social signal, reflecting our personal culture, an expression of who we are, and culinary interests offer a way to redefine our identity, a delicious way to connect.

I take pride and joy in my cooking. There's a happy energy in the kitchen that triggers my endorphins with feelings of competence and confidence, like a runner's high. As a single mom with few relatives, I was always seeking tangible ways to generate a family feeling, and inviting people over for a home-cooked meal became a happy ritual in our household. Those moments carry on the culture and tradition of my own little family, a playbook of everyday life, sober. My daughters learned early on the spirit of hospitality and personal satisfaction of conquering culinary skills, a future asset for sweet home life. Over the years, I've become expert at putting a meal together for four or forty with little notice, and I never worry if there's enough food or room at the table. Cooking for others unlocked new confidence, making me feel whole and safe, solidifying my sobriety.

*****

2004, Hindsight, the Karma of Sobriety

Over the past four decades, I've witnessed a steady trickle of talented people with potential, now dead from drugs. Attending too many funerals, one develops hindsight—call it the karma of sobriety—and after many years, I came to believe sober luck was on my side. I flourished on my recovery journey(s) for fifteen consecutive years for the first time and nearly got it right. Then life happened, and I relapsed, dragging my young children along. Somehow, magically, spiritually, the karma of sobriety transformed an agonizing climb back into a blessing in disguise, as a sober mom, a Hungry Mother. That was over twenty-five years ago, and along with those fifteen years of recovery, adds up to forty years of hindsight.

There are moments I'll write down sobriety dates, a reminder of how all things pass, but nowadays I need a calculator to keep track!

Thank goodness this rational adult, or senior, more like it, trusts what keeps me sober today will work twenty-four hours from now. But why am I compelled to pass along a singular message of hope for mothers in recovery? Because we hold the destiny of our children's mental health in the palm of our hand, and those of their future children, and of generations to come. Embracing recovery gifts us to become the woman, mother, and grandmother we had hoped to be and to pass it on.

The Ying and Yang of bearing twice the responsibility, that of yourself and your children on this journey, yields twice the reward, a serene destination. Hungry Mothers are on a collective journey of recovery, where action plural verbs, "We are," "You are," "They are," and, "I am," can make sustaining sobriety a Herculean effort. And despite the emotional, spiritual, and physical bankruptcy felt each night, our energy is magically, mystically, and maternally restored to us the next morning. I call that a miracle.

Over time, we get to grow into the roles of our lives and live them well. On my timeline, I can visualize the transition from abstinence to early recovery, to seasoned sobriety, and finally, to self-actualization. The natural maturity and wisdom that substance abuse interrupted returns to us. It's the spark—all the perspective, intuition, and accumulated instincts add up to robust energy for whatever we tackle or tickles our fancy. We get to pass along that spark as a joyous song, or for me, as a delicious, belly-humming meal, leading to the collective sigh of satiation at the dinner table. Finally understanding it's not about abstinence, it's a way to serenity. The woman in seasoned sobriety is a woman of conviction, free from the expectations of others, no longer enslaved by addiction, free to pursue a higher calling.

Organically, my sobriety grew into a social conscience. Attending weekly women's meetings for years, I connected with a charismatic lady who brought 12-step meetings to the Nassau County jail women's unit. She cited how incarcerated mothers seemed more motivated, counting the days in prison to be reunited with children, ready to embrace a program of recovery. Hearing me speak, she asked if I was willing to run a group at the jail. That "spark" spoke to me, but I was intimidated by the setting. Snap out of it, girl, I chided myself. Those women could have been you! So, I agreed to pass along a message of hope to women incarcerated for drug use—that it's possible to reconnect with your children by staying sober.

*****

Nassau County Jail

A few months later, after interviews and a clean background check, I arrived at the prison's main entrance, gulping my breath. Naturally, it was raining. I rang the bell, and finally, the gate slid open in slow motion, as if under great weight. It was the weight of tears, remorse, and tragedy waiting inside. Briefed and escorted, I passed through electronic doors and heard them slam shut, louder each time, on the long walk to the unit, passing guards ushering male prisoners in hallways of gloomy gray. At last, I reached the women's pod. They were all in orange jumpsuits seated in a circle with one empty seat, mine. Wait, what? I asked myself. A chair waiting for me in prison? The metaphor was not lost on me, which boosted my commitment and courage.

That was how it started, and over the next two years, I brought mother's groups to treatment programs at Phoenix House, Daytop, and to private community groups on Long Island. Hearing their stories of lost custody and learning the circumstances, I was in awe of their commitment to a recovery program. Many carried outdated photos, lopsided proof of being good moms despite not seeing their children in years. Most were determined to get their kids back or obtain increased visitation; that dream was a beacon of hope.

The ties of motherhood are impossible to extinguish, and I emphatically believe they can be rekindled by embracing recovery. Nearly everything on this earth grows back, so why not the indelible mother-child bond? It's not easy and doesn't happen overnight. All relationships ebb and flow. Be patient, commit to a program, and never give up. Write an email or buy a gift at the Dollar Store with a note that says, I love you. Keep the flame alive with recovery, the truest proof of your willingness to change. Never believe it's over; it never is. Our relationship with our children lasts a lifetime.

*****

Hungry Mother Tips

- Doing for others opens an emotional space for compassion to flourish. We do ourselves the most good by doing for others.
- Family-style meals nurture relationships. Never under-estimate the power of an invitation to dinner, no matter the menu.
- Volunteering increases social interaction. Expand your social network; connect with new people based on common interests. Try it as a family activity!
- A sense of purpose and appreciation brings happy energy. Cooking for others triggers feelings of competence and confidence, like a runner's high. It's yours for the taking.

Benefit Of Cooking

Family dinners around the holidays take on a special meaning all their own. Over the years, each person becomes known for a holiday dish and is counted on to bring. It gives all a chance to contribute and adds to the memories of gathering together.

Hungry Mother Recipe: Holiday Noodle Pudding

10-12 servings

This recipe brings a rich custardy casserole, a staple of Jewish cooking, to the table, as a wonderful side dish. Its sweetness can be enhanced by substituting raisins with any dried (soaked) fruit, from apricots to pineapple, or for a savory taste, switch caramelized onions for fruit.

It's a comforting feeling when family and friends request this dish. In my heart, I hope my recipes outlast my lifetime; in the same way, I cherish recipes from my mother and grandmother today. A wonderful way to be remembered.

Ingredients

1 cup raisins or any combination of dried fruits (apricot, pineapple)
1/4 cup orange juice
1-pound broad (wide) egg noodles (1 package 16 oz.)
8 tbsp unsalted butter, cut into pieces, more for pan
4 large eggs
1 cup cottage cheese
1 cup sour cream
1/3 cup sugar (white or brown)
1 tsp ground cinnamon
Pinch of salt

Directions

1. Put raisins in a microwave-safe bowl or small saucepan and cover with orange juice. Heat on stovetop or in microwave oven until liquid is steaming hot. Let cool.
2. Preheat oven to 400 degrees. Butter a casserole dish.
3. Cook noodles according to package directions and drain well. Immediately return noodles to pot and add butter. Toss until butter melts.
4. In a large bowl, whisk together the eggs, cottage cheese, sour cream, sugar, cinnamon, and salt. Drain raisins and add to bowl along with buttered noodles. Mix well.
5. Spread mixture in prepared pan and smooth top.
6. Bake until top is crusty and golden, 25 to 35 minutes. Serve warm or at room temperature.

Acknowledgments

I am forever thankful and lucky to have had the advice, wisdom, and compassion of these gifted therapists: Dr. Daniel Casriel, Dr. Marc Galanter, and Lew Abrams, and blessed to have crossed paths with Rabbi Abraham Twerksi.

Grateful appreciation to Rabbi Irwin Huberman, co-founder of nerali.org, who encouraged and supported me to follow the conviction of my beliefs for the greater good.

And to Cheryl Benton, publisher, who skillfully detangled and ironed out my story to make the *Hungry Mother* happen.

About The Author

When Jane Fox left the wealthy enclave she grew up in on Long Island and headed for college in the '70s, she fell into the counter culture's easy access to drugs, leading to her addiction. She was in and out of recovery programs, finally getting sober at AREBA Casriel Institute in New York City in 1976. She never lost touch with the recovery community and had many active roles in the industry, including that of TV spokesperson, appearing on the *Oprah, Donohue*, and *Regis* shows.

Yet no one is immune. After fifteen years sober, and now a divorced mom with two young children, she relapsed. It was the climb back and hosting See Jane Cook (CNBC) that inspired the writing of *Hungry Mother*. The art of eating and cooking has always been a central theme in Jane's life, and she sustained her sobriety by incorporating culinary activities into a simple yet revolutionary approach to long-term recovery. That was over twenty-five years ago, and since then, Jane has been on a mission to "pass it on" to other mothers in recovery.

Jane Fox is a New York State Certified Recovery Peer Advocate and co-founder of nerali.org, a sobriety resource for the Long Island Jewish community. She brings the depth of her experience from living on both sides of the sobriety fence to support groups for family members with a loved one struggling with sobriety. She advocates for structured culinary workshops to be integrated into recovery programs. Learn more at thehungrymothers.com.

Made in the USA
Middletown, DE
31 October 2022

13780836R00084